Perceiving and Behaving

Perceiving and Behaving

DALE G. LAKE

TEACHERS COLLEGE PRESS
Teachers College, Columbia University
NEW YORK, NEW YORK

Preface

What do dissertations accomplish for the learner, and for the world? They are supposed to initiate the graduate student into the world of "serious" research: yet the *modal* number of research publications for all those holding the doctorate is zero. They are supposed to contribute to "knowledge": yet most dissertations go unread and unsung. Why should this be?

Two major reasons occur to me. In most graduate schools the dissertation is a hurdle, a barrier to be managed with the minimum effort consistent with self-esteem and the approval of powerful evaluators. Thus it does not *lead* anywhere, but becomes an end in itself. Second, the "hurdle" character of the dissertation interacts powerfully with certain intellectual styles in particular academic fields, pressing the student to choose variables which are familiar, instruments which are convenient, and questions which are safety "controllable" (i.e., narrow, parochial, simplistic, mechanical).

Dissertations need not be like this. They can be carried out as satisfying experiences, which lead to further satisfying experiences in the world of knowledge-making. And they can criticize and expand the compartmentalized, self-confirming world of academic intellectual fashions.

Dale Lake's work is a case in point, more so than any dissertation I have had contact with in the past decade. I commend it not only to students and faculty in psychology, but to anyone who is toying with the idea that research in graduate schools should deal with meaningful problems and be carried out in a meaningful manner. It is no surprise that the study won an Honorable Mention in the national Creative Talent Awards competition sponsored by the American Institutes of Research in 1966.

I would like to underline some important features of the work. First, it is holistic, refusing a bivariate, billiard-ball view of man. What happens in an interpersonal situation is seen as a function of the perceiver, the perceived, and the situation itself. Many social psychologists have explored one term or another of this equation; very few have managed to explore them all in the systematic way that Lake has.

Second, Lake's design is beautifully congruent with the conclusions he reached from a very thorough and integrative review of the relevant literature. "Accuracy" of perception, he suggests, has been extensively explored (because of convenience?), with little resulting fruit. The issue, in life as in the laboratory, is: what consequences do our perceptions of others have for our behavior towards them, and how do our perceptions and behavior change over time?

Third, as would be expected, the study takes a *processual* view of experimental design, following its subjects through a series of events: forming impressions of others; acting towards others; receiving, confirming, or disconfirming information about others; behaving in new ways as a result. All these events, as in life, occur in flux, over time, *not* in a marked-off point in space-time. This design also permitted thoughtful explorations of the relations among all these events (i.e., processes), rather than restricting Lake to isolated, trivial statements of relationships "between X and Y, all other things being equal."

Finally, the results make sense. Good science brings us coherence, not hazily qualified assertions which waver when their methodological underpinnings are poked at. Lake shows us that the intentions of parties to a bargaining situation do make a difference, that our personality dispositions to be manipulative or collaborative are crucial in guiding our views of others and our own behavioral style, and that learning something you had not expected about someone else alters—slowly or quickly—how you relate to him. Generalizations of this sort are useful at bargaining tables in the real world, *and* in the social psychology laboratory. We need many more such studies.

Graduate students traditionally make acknowledgements to professors. In this case, I would like to thank Dale Lake for the way in which he expanded my vision of appropriate inquiry in the domain he chose.

Matthew B. Miles

Acknowledgements

I wish to acknowledge with thanks the many who made possible the successful completion of this study. Specifically deserving of mention are:

The social psychology students of Teachers College who patiently helped me in three oral presentations of my design ideas. Deserving special mention are Harvey Hornstein, Dan Callahan, Pete Gumpert, Ella Lasky, and Yakov Epstein for their many hours of help on design, laboratory work and statistical analysis.

Professors Deutsch and Christie for creating departments of social psychology where student-faculty interaction is not a sterile classroom activity but is rather a total educational experience.

My wife, Gerry, for her constant support and encouragement.

And to Professor Miles whose encouragement, criticisms, reactions and attention to details made the entire project a learning experience rather than a bureaucratic requirement, I offer my deepest appreciation.

These efforts are dedicated to the memory of my father, Charles W. Lake (d. 1965), whose early demise kept him from seeing the fruition of his labors.

Dale G. Lake
State University of New York at Albany

Contents

Appendixes

Tables and Figures

Perceiving and Behaving

I

An Orientation to Interpersonal Perception

THE AREA OF DISCOURSE

Definitions

The psychology of the processes whereby one person comes to know and to think about an Other person has no satisfactory label. The problem area has been variously called: person perception, interpersonal perception, impression formation, person apperception, the ability to judge people, etc.

Of course the labels are not important: what they represent is. It is safe to say that the label "perception" as it has been classically used does not represent the process typically described in a person perception study. The classical use of the term perception, coming from psychophysics, indicates that when a given energy level surpasses the appropriate sensory mechanism's threshold, the individual becomes aware of the energy emission. Given this definition of perception, one may either not use the term in referring to the process of coming to know an Other, or one may reject the definition. The research literature shows that the latter choice has typically been made, although some do prefer to call the process cognition. Rejecting the definition is justified; for as Bruner and Postman have shown,[1] it is clear that selectivity in awareness is difficult, if not impossible, to eliminate.

Whatever the label, most researchers will agree that the process of coming to know an Other human involves more than mere threshold awareness. For instance Bruner has argued that the process of perception tends, in general, to accomplish two things: 1) "a recoding of the diversity of data we encounter into a simpler form that brings it within the scope of our limited memory; 2) a going beyond the information given to predict future events and thereby minimize surprise."[2] Tagiuri's definition is similar: "We propose using the term person

---

[1] J. S. Bruner & L. Postman, Perception, cognition and behavior. *J. Pers.*, 1949, 18, 14–31.

[2] J. S. Bruner, Going beyond the information given. In Jessor, *et al.* (Eds.), *A Symposium on Cognition*. Cambridge: Harvard University Press, 1957.

perception whenever the *perceiver regards the object as having the potential of representation and intentionality* . . . we refer mostly to observations we make about *intentions, attitudes, emotions, ideas, abilities, purposes, traits* – events that are, so to speak, inside the person." [3]

Osgood suggests that there is even more to perception.

> Social perception involves the organization of information about persons and the *attribution of properties* to them, often on the basis of only sketchy cues. These properties manifest *constancy*, in spite of observed variations, and are *selectively* attributed in the sense that they are influenced by the perceiver's psychological states. The processes by which information is organized are *flexible*; the same body of information is subject to patterning in different ways. Thus social perception refers to a set of processes that intervene between the presentation of information about a person and awareness of him. [4]

Examination of the literature shows that Osgood's definition most nearly covers the range of phenomena discussed in person perception studies, so it is most adequate as a definition. However, the other terms – person perception, interpersonal perception, etc. – can be used interchangeably as long as the phenomena being studied are clear.

Research Problems

Research problems follow quite naturally from the above definitions of person perception. First, and most often studied, are the constellations of phenomena revolving around *the person doing the perceiving*. Studies in this area are myriad. A representative (but not exhaustive) list would include studies of: accuracy in perceiving the Other; age, sex, and intelligence of the perceiver; and self-insight, cognitive complexity, social skill, and psychological adjustment of the perceiver. Additionally, personality orientations such as authoritarianism, rigidity, field independence versus field dependence, repression versus sensitization, have been examined.

A second line of investigation includes studies which either directly or indirectly examine the *characteristics of those perceived*. In these studies different perceived populations are compared on the same task, or specific sub-populations are selected to be perceived, as in perceptions of Negro versus white populations. Other studies prefer to examine the effects of the perceived's role or status upon perception. Still other studies attempt to alter certain physical characteristics of the person being perceived, such as his smile or his frown, in order to see what emotions can be portrayed with physical features.

---

[3] R. Tagiuri, Introduction. In R. Tagiuri & L. Petrullo (Eds.), *Person perception and interpersonal behavior*. Stanford: Stanford University Press, 1958.

[4] C. E. Osgood, *Method and theory in experimental psychology*. New York: Oxford University Press, 1953, p. 34.

The type of study which occurs least often in the literature is the one devoted to an investigation of the *situation* in which a perception of the Other person is formed. Early studies in this area usually altered the perceptual field with special rooms or lenses. More recent studies have examined the effects of changing the motivational structure for forming impressions.

The dilemmas of research in person perception become immediately obvious. Which of the three aspects – the perceiver, the perceived, or the situation – should be held constant while the others are manipulated? Is it really possible methodologically to hold the perceiver *and* the situation constant while manipulating the perceived? Are there any constancies or generalizations that may be made about perceivers across situations and persons perceived? What theories are available which adequately help to generate testable hypotheses for the researcher interested in person perception?

These questions raise two sets of implications for a thorough literature review. First, a representative sample of studies *within* each of the areas – the perceiver, the perceived, and the situation, needs to be undertaken. Second, phenomena *common* to more than one area need to be examined. This requires extensive integration of studies from each of the areas in order to discover whether there are generic trends which would suggest person perception hypotheses not limited to a particular area or experimental design. Thus, the review of the literature in this paper is more comprehensive than is typical of a study looking at only one of the three areas.

In the rest of this chapter selected research studies will be discussed which have attempted to understand one or more of the above areas. One should be cautioned, however, that the assignment of any particular study to the perceiver, perceived, or situation aspect must at times be arbitrary; obviously investigators may study more than one aspect at a time.

The Perceiver

In forming an impression of an Other, the perceiver attributes specific traits to the stimulus person; he forms feelings of like or dislike, respect, etc. He organizes the information he receives about the Other into an impression. These may be impressions about the Other's actions, whether they are caused by some situational factor or whether they are intentionally performed. What must be known about the perceiver in order to know how he forms an impression?

Accuracy. Judging from the amount of research that has been done, one might conclude that accuracy in forming impressions of Others is an important phenomenon. Accuracy is typically measured by one of two methods, both of which have serious shortcomings. One method employs a comparison between subjects' predictions of how a stimulus person will fill out an inventory and how the person actually fills it out. The other method involves a comparison between a subject's description of a stimulus person and the mean of all subjects' descriptions of that person.

The first method, involving one judge and a stimulus person, usually results in the contamination of response sets and the influence of the unknown factors that mediate responses to an inventory, and is also a task which is of questionable relevance to the perception of persons, unless one is specifically interested in the ability of one person to predict Others' modes of self-presentation.

Taft reviewed the research concerning the ability to judge other people. He was able to conclude very little. For instance, in respect to age of the perceiver, he makes the judgment, "While ability to judge emotional expression increases with age in children . . . no increase with age has been found in adults on various tests of ability to judge others." [5] In regard to sex he is even less certain, "The weight of evidence is in favor of no sex differences in ability to judge or perhaps a slightly superior ability in women." [6] Other interesting and equally tenuous conclusions are:

Physical scientists, and possibly other non-psychologists, e.g., personnel workers, appear to be more capable of judging others accurately than are either psychology students or clinical psychologists. [7]

Ability to judge others on analytic modes correlates positively with emotional adjustment. [8]

Persons who show insight into their own status with respect to their peers on individual traits tend to also rate their peers accurately on those traits. [9]

The ability to predict how others will respond to opinion items shows a consistent positive relationship with measures of social skill, such as leadership, salesmanship and popularity. [10]

Given the tenuousness of these judgments, about the only conclusion one might confidently make is that there seem to be individual differences in the ability to judge other people. Cronbach[11] destroys even this confidence. He sees two difficulties with the measures typically used in the studies of the type reviewed by Taft. First, if the empathy, i.e., the ability to judge an Other, of one judge is significantly greater than the empathy of a second, the difference in scores may be due to great differences in judging certain of the dimensions which underlie

---

[5] R. Taft, The ability to judge people, *Psychol. Bull.*, 52, 1955, 7.

[6] *Ibid.*, p. 8.

[7] *Ibid.*, p. 12.

[8] *Ibid.*, p. 14.

[9] *Ibid.*, p. 17.

[10] *Ibid.*, p. 19.

[11] L. J. Cronbach, Processes affecting scores on "understanding of others" and "assumed similarity." *Psychol. Bull.*, 1955, 52, 177–194.

the questionnaire; while on other dimensions there may be no difference at all. For example, if a factor analysis were done of scores on a certain test, and a large number of dimensions were extracted, it might well be that judges would be very good at estimating the scores of other persons on certain of these dimensions and not on others. Cronbach's first objection is that investigators are not apt to do a refined analysis of the empathy scores, but are likely to assume that the greater empathy (or accuracy) of one group of judges is generalized across all the dimensions of the test. The second objection Cronbach has to the overall measurement of empathic ability is the converse of this; namely, that the overall accuracy scores of two sets of judges may be virtually equal yet one set of judges could be far more accurate on certain of these dimensions which underlie the test. However, the greater accuracy on these dimensions could be submerged in a general score taken over all dimensions.

The third and most important difficulty that Cronbach finds with a measure of this sort is that it is difficult to know what one is measuring. Suppose, as in the above example, the one set of judges shows significantly greater accuracy in estimating the responses of a group of people than does a second set of judges. One would like to say that this shows that the first set of judges was more attuned to the personalities of the people rated; that is, the first set of judges was either better able to perceive cues which the objects emitted, or was better able to valuate the cues it did perceive. However, this may not be the case at all.

Rather, it may be that the final accuracy score would reflect only the characteristics of the judges. For example, the judge might project his own beliefs, attitudes and personality mechanisms upon everyone with whom he came in contact. He would then rate every object as giving answers similar to those he, the judge, would give if he were taking the test. If the subjects did happen to be similar to him in personality, then he would get a high accuracy score; but this would be quite fortuitous. And here there was no interaction between the judge and the stimulus object; that is, the characteristics of the object and the cues he emitted were largely irrelevant to the judge's ratings.

The unfortunate thing about the accuracy score is, thus, that it offers no way for the investigator to tell whether the accuracy scores achieved by judges are due to some sort of interaction or are due primarily to the characteristics of the judges. Research reviewed subsequently in this study has also established that there are characteristics of the judges other than a tendency to project one's own personality traits upon those one perceives, which can, given a favorable choice of subjects, lead to high scores on empathy without the judges having been influenced by the cues the object emitted.

Another major difficulty with the accuracy score is that artifacts very easily arise which confuse the interpretation of the data. This occurs, in part, because two measures which are based upon the same data are often correlated with each other. For example, one might ask whether secure therapists perceive their clients as more similar to themselves in security than do insecure therapists. The usual procedure is to correlate scores (security and assumed similarity) which, being derived from the same instrument, are not mathematically independent. Thus, high correlations must automatically ensue since the two measures are not based upon independent sets of data. This measurement procedure becomes particularly dangerous when certain of the basic data are unreliable, since errors in measurement are then transmitted to both of the measures which are correlated.

Finally, Cronbach contends that any time a heterogeneous set of items is combined into a single global index, certain artifacts will typically follow. For instance, the effect measured by the global index may be interpreted as general overall content in the instrument, when it is actually due to one or two prominent dimensions. Another problem arises in that "a relation that is too weak to be significant when tested on one dimension might reach significance if strengthened by combining several dimensions. If this is the case, however, then the relation could be brought to significance for some of the separate dimensions by employing more reliable measures or more subjects." [12]

Research illustration. Altrocchi[13] gives an excellent research example of the validity of Cronbach's criticism of global indices. The global index considered is that of assumed similarity or dissimilarity. The measure consists of squaring the difference between the judge's estimate of the object on each item and the judge's estimate of himself. This figure is then summed over all the items in the test. The lower the score, the more the judge sees the object as similar to himself — his assumed similarity. Altrocchi asked the research question, "Do sensitizers assume more dissimilarity than repressors between self and other in interpersonal perception?" [14] He also proposed to analyze the data as Gordon[15] had, and according to recommendations offered by Cronbach above.

In the first analysis with the lumped assumed dissimilarity scores, he found that sensitizers were significantly more likely to assume dissimilarity than repressors.[16] But, using the Cronbach method of component analysis, he found that the highly significant differences were due to two of the *monadic components* — differences in means and standard deviations of their self-concepts. Thus, "there was little evidence that either repressors or sensitizers

[12] L. J. Cronbach, Proposals leading to analytic treatment of social perception scores. In R. Taguiri & L. Petrullo (Eds.), *Person perception and interpersonal behavior.* Stanford University Press, 1958. p. 362.

[13] J. Altrocchi, Interpersonal perceptions of repressors and sensitizers and component analysis of assumed dissimilarity scores. *J. abnorm. soc. Psychol.,* 1961, 62, 528–535. (From time to time a single study such as this one will be used to illustrate general methodological trends.)

[14] *Ibid.*

[15] J. E. Gordon, The stability of the assumed similarity response set in repressors and sensitizers. *J. Pers.,* 1959, 27, 362–373.

[16] J. Altrocchi, *loc. cit.*

tended to base their descriptions of others on their descriptions of themselves – and thus little evidence of a dyadic phenomenon – and no clear evidence that the groups tended to differ significantly in their perception of others." [17] Thus, the differences in the first analysis were due primarily to stable differences in self-description, and not to any clear difference in perception of others' self-description nor to any substantial correlation between perception of others and perception of self.

Measuring accuracy. It is clear then that the typical methods of measuring accuracy involve the contamination of response sets and influence of the unknown factors that mediate responses to an inventory, in the method in which judges are asked to "perceive" how an Other might complete a questionnaire. In the other method in which a judge's description of an Other is compared with the mean of all subjects' descriptions of that person, the effect of regression to the mean is that the person with the highest accuracy score is the one who most accurately judges the responses of the judging group.

Despite these problems, Cronbach in 1958 was still optimistic. He saw the whole field of person perception as advancing to a state of perfection. He was convinced that research was reaching the point where, "the problem is stated more rigorously, often by means of a mathematical model connecting in an orderly way the phenomena which previously caused confusion and error." [18] Either history has proven him wrong, or the process of "emerging" is a long one. While there have been recent attempts at more precise quantifications, e.g., Jackson and Messick's[19] description of some possible linkages between mathematical scaling models on the one hand and concrete problems in the area of person cognition on the other, the problems remain. In fact, the measurement problems may be even more complicated than Cronbach suggested. In a recent article, Ager and Dawes[20] found evidence demonstrating that persons may be able to make judgments about Others' attitudes more easily on the end of the attitude scale which is similar to their own orientation. Thus, the authors, in a linear trend analysis, showed that pro-science subjects had significantly more confusions among the less favorable, non-science categories, the reverse being true for the anti-science group. If this proves to be a general finding, then any accuracy score which assumes equal scale intervals will be artifactual.

The research on accuracy is simply a mine-field of artifacts and errors which is, for even the most intrepid and optimistic investigator, reason to tread cautiously, if not to become immobilized. And there is evidence that immobilization is present. Shrauger and Altrocchi comment, "Despite attempts

[17] *Ibid.,* p. 531–2.
[18] L. J. Cronbach, Proposals leading to analytic treatment of social perception scores.
[19] D. N. Jackson & S. Messick, Individual differences in social perception. *Brit. J. soc. clin. Psychol.,* 1963, 2, 1.
[20] J. W. Ager & F. M. Dawes, The effect of judges' attitudes on judgment. *J. Pers. soc. Psychol.,* 1965, 1, 533–539.

to refine measures of accuracy, one cannot, on the basis of current research evidence, be assured that people at one extreme on any personality dimension are consistently more prone to perceive specific kinds of other people more accurately than are people at the other extreme." [21] Secord and Backman add, "Unfortunately, the assessment of accuracy has raised such difficult methodological problems that the definitive research necessary to provide conclusive answers to these questions has not yet been carried out." [22]

This review of the measurement literature concerning accuracy has shown that generally the results are equivocal. And yet, one of the major questions most often asked in research on accuracy – "In what dimensions is accuracy a general ability, and in what dimensions not general?" – must still be reviewed. Keeping in mind the previously discussed measurement problems, what can be said in response to this question?

Accuracy as a general ability. Crow and Hammond[23] criticize previous studies of interpersonal perception for assuming generality of interpersonal perceptiveness when no such trait has been established empirically. To support their argument, they devised two studies: the first to investigate generality of interpersonal perceptiveness over different procedures, controlling statistically for response sets; the second to investigate the generality of accuracy over time. They suggest that Cronbach's method of getting a differential accuracy score is not really applicable to this type of study, because it is a parametric technique and, therefore, assumes a normal distribution of the dependent and independent variables. In the first study, they constructed a series of tasks involving judgments, and after computing differential accuracy scores for each individual on each task and working out a correlation matrix, they found that only eight out of 105 possible correlations among the fifteen measures were significant beyond the five percent level. Crow and Hammond conclude that although it is possible that generality may be demonstrated using other procedures or other judges, the negative results make the assumption of generality untenable.

In a second study, senior medical students who saw sound film interviews of patients at three six-month intervals were asked to estimate the patients' responses to personality scales. Differential accuracy was determined as in the first study, and three response sets were studied. Crow and Hammond concluded that: stereotypes are stable response sets. Accuracy is not. Consistency over time may be due to consistency in response sets, rather than to consistency in interpersonal perceptiveness. Crow and Hammond doubt the reliability of studies demonstrating generality which have not been controlled for response sets.

[21] S. Shrauger & J. Altrocchi, The personality of the perceiver as a factor in person perception. *Psychol. Bull.*, 1964, 62, 291.

[22] P. F. Secord & C. W. Backman, *Social Psychology* New York: McGraw-Hill, 1964, p. 79.

[23] W. J. Crow & K. R. Hammond, The generality of accuracy and response sets in interpersonal perception. *J. abnorm. soc. Psychol.*, 1957, 54, 384–396.

Cline and Richards[24] criticize Crow and Hammond's findings on the latter's use of an odd scoring technique, in that they eliminated stereotype accuracy by calling it a response set rather than considering it as a component of accuracy. They promptly set out to demonstrate that accuracy is a general skill. Cline and Richards used ten color and sound films of interviews concerning entirely different stimulus persons from the ones used by Crow and Hammond. There was a great deal more variety in the stimulus persons, who included: a nineteen year-old male geology major, a sixty-five year-old widow, a single Mexican-American working in a meat-packing plant, and seven others. The judges were college students. The instruments included standardized personality inventories, word associations, sentence completions, and trait ratings. All the instruments had been responded to by the interviewee.

The results suggest that accuracy in judging others is a general skill. The accuracy scores for each test were correlated with the scores for each other test with a range of .30 to .65. They concluded that accuracy in perceiving others is a general ability, but a general ability that can be analyzed into two independent components: stereotype accuracy and differential or interpersonal accuracy. Their results, however, still leave the question, "general over what dimensions?" unanswered. The differences between their findings and Crow's (ignoring procedural differences for the moment) might be in the content of the filmed interviews, since they were more related to the task of perecption by the judges than the films in the Cline and Richards study. Also, Cline and Richards allowed their subjects to review the instruments briefly prior to seeing the films, which may have helped tune them for the task.

O'Connor[25] criticized Cline and Richards' technique for reducing the number of films which were the stimuli for the act of perception. Cline and Richards admitted that they "to a certain extent 'stack the cards' in favor of a general trait," [26] by eliminating the films on the basis of the extent to which they discriminated between good judges and poor judges. In their defense of this procedure, they suggest that this process is essentially a standard item analysis. O'Connor says this is faulty logic, since a similar logic could be employed to support a directly opposite approach. He says, "The use of item analysis procedures which minimize item-total co-variance values would admittedly introduce a bias in favor of finding specificity in judging ability." [27]

Cline and Richards[28] agree with his criticism, but not his conclusion. They state that O'Connor is correct, in that items could be selected to define a

---

[24] V. B. Cline & J. M. Richards, Jr., Accuracy of interpersonal perception: a general trait? *J. abnorm. soc. Psychol.*, 1960, 60, 1–7.

[25] W. F. O'Connor, A methodological note on the Cline and Richards' studies on accuracy of interpersonal perception. *J. abnorm. soc. Psychol.*, 1963, 66, 194–195.

[26] Cline & Richards, *op. cit.*, p. 17.

[27] W. F. O'Connor, *op. cit.*, p. 195.

[28] V. B. Cline & J. M. Richards, Jr., Cline and Richards' reply to O'Connor's methodological note. *J. abnorm. soc. Psychol.*, 1963, 66, 195.

heterogeneous scale. But they are still of the opinion that their results suggest *"that a homgeneous scale of accuracy of interpersonal perception will be found if a methodology appropriate to the definition of a homogeneous scale is used."*[29] Further, "The authors suspect that the underlying difficulty is that their procedure is necessary, but not sufficient for the definition of a *meaningful* homogeneous scale. In other words, the authors succeeded in establishing a reliable scale, but it is still to be demonstrated that their instrument has 'construct validity.'"[30] Whether accuracy is or is not a general or specific skill is still in question.

Cline and Richards have raised problems of reliability and validity. These are really the basic problems in all of the accuracy studies reviewed. The controversies over generality versus specificity, and over what is the best way to obtain accuracy scores, are both reliability questions. No one has bothered to ask "accuracy for what?" Of what value is it to be able to show that it is not clear whether any particular group of persons is better at *guessing* how an Other will respond to an MMPI or EPPS scale? Notice that all the studies considered so far have used paper and pencil criterion measures in determining accuracy. Perhaps it should be pointed out that all the paper and pencil instruments were constructed by psychologists who, as we learned in the article by Taft,[31] were the most inaccurate of all the adult populations sampled. But, what are the behavioral consequences of a specific perception?

This further confounding of the problem – making subjects respond to dimensions selected by the experimenter, and not validating accuracy on criteria other than paper and pencil instruments – needs to be discussed.

Person perception as a free response. Hastorf, Richardson, and Dornbusch[32] suggest that the studies of person perception would make more headway if they met the following two criteria: "Researchers should make more of an attempt to study the perceptual categories that are actually employed by, and thus relevant to, the perceiver under consideration. . . . Studies of perception *made by social psychologists* should always have at the forefront the relationship of the perceptual act under consideration to some other aspect of the social behavior of the perceiver."[33]

Further, they recommend a momentary pause in the search for the "trait" of sensitivity in order to study the qualities of a person's experience of others in terms of the verbal categories he uses in reporting that experience. Two studies have since been conducted in accordance with their recommendations.

---

[29] *Ibid.*, p. 193.

[30] *Ibid.*, p. 196.

[31] R. Taft, *op. cit.*, p. 1–23.

[32] A. H. Hastorf, S. A. Richardson & S. M. Dornbusch, The problem of relevance in the study of person perception. In R. Tagiuri & L. Petrullo (Eds.), *Person perception and interpersonal behavior.* Stanford: Stanford University Press, 1958, p. 54–63.

[33] *Ibid.,* p. 58.

Research illustrations. Beach and Wertheimer consider the general research question in studies of person perception to be: "What kinds of dimensions are used by different kinds of subjects when describing different kinds of others under different kinds of conditions?" [34] Given this as a task, they asked college students to describe twelve others within assigned classifications they thought of themselves. The descriptions were categorized into four major dimensions: objective information, social interaction, behavioral consistencies, and performance and activities.

After developing a set of initial content categories, efforts were made to obtain respectable inter-judge reliability; when this was done, an examination of the way different subjects described different Others in one situation was undertaken. The results suggest that in one situation it is possible to categorize subjects' descriptions of Others adequately enough; that the differences between subjects, the differences between Others, and the effects of various interactions between subject and Other variables can be shown to produce significant differences in category use, evaluative tone of the descriptions, and the amount of information given in descriptions. Further, the authors suggest that when selecting scales or dimensions upon which the subject is to be required to make judgments about Others, one must keep in mind that these dimensions are not going to be applicable to all Others and subjects.

It may be that a subject responds randomly to dimensions which are inappropriate for him, which might help to explain some of the erratic findings in the studies reviewed earlier. The authors also suggest, "in an accuracy experiment it may be necessary to find those dimensions which the Other considers appropriate to himself." [35]

This study still doesn't deal with the validity problem. That is, why are the subjects describing their perceptions of Others in this experiment? Why, of course, because the experimenters *want* them to. So this still doesn't help to insure that the perceptions as described would have meaning for behavior in other types of situations. Also, the authors do not discuss some obvious measurement problems in their categorization system. For instance, each subject had one page for one description and yet an "amount of information" category was used in which females "tended to be somewhat more productive than males." Is this a sex difference or a size of writing difference? Further, how does the subjects' verbal ability interact with the content coding system? Regardless of these unanswered questions, this investigation looks promising.

Hastorf, Dornbusch, *et al.*[36] report the first analysis of an experiment similar to that of Beach and Wertheimer. However, there are some important differences

---

[34] L. Beach & M. A. Wertheimer, A free response approach to the study of person cognition. *J. abnorm. soc. Psychol.*, 1961, 62, 368.

[35] *Ibid.*, p. 373.

[36] A. H. Hastorf, S. M. Dornbusch, *et al.*, The perceiver and the perceived: Their relative influence on the categories of interpersonal cognition. *J. Pers. soc. Psychol.*, 1965, 1, 434.

in methodology. First, they use children as their subjects. Their content analysis is carefully constructed to reflect as nearly as possible the actual categories used by the children. The responses of the subjects were collected with open-end interviews, in which the subject was asked to describe another person in an outdoor camp. Hastorf, Dornbusch, *et al.* introduce the notion that with the freedom to respond which the subject has in this experiment, one ought to be able to develop measures of the subject's own salience in category use. Two such indices of salience are developed. The initial results show that overlap in category use is greatest when the same perceiver is describing two Others, next greatest when two perceivers are describing an Other, and least when two describers are describing two Others. The crucial questions for person perception await further data analysis. "Are there certain categories that appear to be mainly perceiver-determined, wheras others may be mainly a function of the perceived? How does category usage vary with one's own interpersonal attraction to that person? Does category usage shift when a liked and a disliked Other are described, or does one merely shift position on category continua? Do people who behave aggressively talk a lot about aggression in their descriptions of Others?" [37]

The study by Hastorf, Dornbusch, *et al.* represents a considerable improvement both in the conceptual and methodological approach to the study of person perception; they are still sensitizing the subject to the *process* of perceiving an Other in a way that is typically not symptomatic of the real world. That is, impressions of Others are usually formed *incidentally* to an ongoing activity. It is the contention here that this incidental process needs to be reflected in the research on persons perceiving Others. Before this point can be developed more fully, however, attention must be directed to the role of the perceived and the role of the situation in studies of person perception.

The Perceived

As was indicated earlier, studies which focus upon the perceived are not as numerous as those of the perceiver. The reasons for this are not entirely obvious. Why is it more interesting to know how an authoritarian perceives an Other than to know how an authoritarian is perceived by an Other? Why are theories of impression formation really theories of reception formation? Some of the following studies will show that important phenomena can be overlooked by concentrating on the perceiver.

For instance, Cantril[38] had experimented with the Ames distorted room for years and had shown that when the perceiver looks at two Others whose heads

---

[37] *Ibid.,* p. 440.

[38] H. Cantril, Perception and interpersonal relations. In E. P. Hollander and R. G. Hunt (Eds.), *Current perspectives in social psychology.* New York: Oxford University Press, 1963, p. 294.

are framed by windows, the head of one individual appears to be very large and the head of the other appears very small to the perceiver. One morning he showed the room to a married couple; the wife was unable to perceive any distortion in her husband's head. This phenomenon was dubbed the "Honi phenomenon." While Cantril goes on to discuss the characteristics of the perceiver which operate in the Honi phenomenon, the point is that it was the relationship of the perceiver to the *perceived* which altered the perceiver's processes.

Order and contrast effects in presenting the Other. Investigators in the field of psychophysics have spent considerable energy studying the order in which objects are presented. In the psychology of persuasion, the order of arguments presented is often a determining factor. Why shouldn't similar effects be present for the order in which the stimulus person – the Other – is presented?

Holmes and Berkowitz maintain that order effects are important. They hypothesize that: "an anchorage or standard is formed on the basis of the experience with the first person and that subsequently, contrast occurs in the perception of the second stranger when there is a great perceived difference between the two." [39] By varying the order in which a "belligerent psychologist," "friendly psychologist," and student were presented as objects to be perceived, they found:

> The presumed comparison person affected the evaluations of at least the male student on both measuring instruments (an adjective check list and a modified social distance scale). The latter stimulus person received the most favorable evaluations when the subjects were given the experience with the "belligerent psychologist" as a comparison and they were asked to judge the student before they judged the second, neutral psychologist. Similarly, he was evaluated most unfavorably when the subjects were provided with the "friendly psychologist" as the anchorage and then heard the student's voice before they heard the voice of the second psychologist. In both instances there is a contrast effect, which apparently is sharpest when the extreme cases follow in succession. [40]

One can only wonder whether contrast effects were operant in the studies reported earlier by Crow-Hammond and Cline-Richards. Certainly the experimental situation of making a series of judgments on different interviewees would be conducive to contrast effects.

Another implication of the Holmes and Berkowitz study is that there may be other contrast effects working in the person perception study. For instance, in addition to contrasting one stimulus person with another, a subject may also contrast himself with a different stimulus person. In fact, it is just possible that

---

[39] D. S. Holmes & L. Berkowitz, Some contrast effects in social perception. *J. abnorm. soc. Psychol.*, 1961, 62, 150.

[40] *Ibid.*, p. 151.

this latter effect may be one of the central organizing activities in person perception. If it is, it also raises some design problems, because for any given subject, any particular stimulus person may be more or less similar to the subject. Thus, the subject may be confident in judgments concerning one class of stimulus persons, whereas he may be only guessing for another type of stimulus person. This problem suggests the need for designs in which the subject familiarizes himself with a given universe of information until he knows how characteristic or uncharacteristic the information is of *himself,* after which he learns where the stimulus person stands on the same information, and then is asked to make a judgment about the stimulus person in relation to a criterion measure which is relevant to the information presented.

Communicating facial expression. Another area of person perception studies which has typically ignored the role of the stimulus person is that characterized by studies which ask a subject to describe what emotion is being portrayed by a static photo. After the subject has indicated what emotion he thinks has been expressed, the variance in recognizability of emotions is sought either in the characteristics of the judge or in the nature of the emotion portrayed. In fact, if a review of these studies were to be undertaken, it would have appeared in the earlier section of this paper entitled "the perceiver." These studies were not reviewed earlier and will not be reviewed here because they are doubtful significance. As Bruner and Tagiuri indicate:

> All in all, one wonders about the significance of "facial expression of emotion": in isolation. From the point of view of the adaptiveness of social behavior, it is rare to the vanishing point that judgment ever takes place on the basis of a face caught in a state similar to that provided by a photograph snapped at 20 milliseconds. Historically speaking, we may have been done a disservice by the pioneering efforts of those who, like Darwin, took the human face in a state of arrested animation as an adequate stimulus situation for studying how well we recognize human emotion.[41]

Similarly, Thompson and Meltzer conclude: "Imagine the consequences for social relations if we always showed anger whenever we felt angry, or if we could not express interest when bored!" [42] In the Thompson and Meltzer study[43] the authors examined the role of the stimulus person in the facial expression type of study. They were not concerned with the recognition of "natural" or "biological" emotional expression, but rather with the success of stimulus persons to make the perceiver feel that the stimulus expressed a particular

---

[41] J. S. Bruner & R. Tagiuri, The perception of people. In G. Lindzey (Ed.), *Handbook of social psychology.* Vol. 2. Cambridge, Mass.: Addison-Wesley, 1954. p. 638.

[42] D. F. Thompson & L. Meltzer, Communication of emotional intent by facial expression. *J. abnorm. soc. Psychol.,* 1964, 68, 129.

[43] *Ibid.,* p. 129–135.

emotion. In this study 50 persons volunteered and were told that their task was to portray by their facial expressions – to four judges – the emotions named on cards they were given.

The results indicate that the expressors "succeeded in communicating to the judges their emotional intent in over 3/5 of the trials, whereas chance success would be 1 out of 10. The least frequently recognized emotion, contempt, was identified correctly in 38% of the trials; at the other extreme, happiness was identified correctly in 76% of the trials." [44]

The expressors were given an enactment score which is the total number of correct judgments of the expressor's two enactments of a particular emotion made by the four judges. The results indicate that out of a possible score of 80, expressors ranged from 69 to 17 and 24 for the two least successful subjects. The expressors also differed in the particular emotions they enacted most effectively. Essentially no relationship was found between an expressor's ability to express any particular emotion and his score on any scale of the California Personality Inventory.

The authors conclude their experiment: "There is also a need to supplement the interest of earlier research in the judge and his characteristics with new research focusing upon the expressors of emotion, their characteristics, and the cues which they produce in attempts to communicate impressions of themselves to others."[45]

If researchers in person perception were to respond to this conclusion, it would result in some radical revisions of experimental design. And this is exactly what Egon Brunswik[46] has indicated, much earlier, needs to be done. He claims that the stimuli responded to in an experiment must be sampled representatively from their universe, just as the subjects who do the responding must be sampled from theirs. His logic is straightforward. Because there are individual differences among people, (he assumes) we would never try to generalize experimental results to "people in general" (or even "college sophomores" in general) on the basis of data from one subject. Accordingly, to the extent that we want to generalize not only to people, but also to "situations," we must sample a variety of situations to use as stimuli.

Brunswik actually carried out a study on perceptual size constancy to illustrate just these arguments. *One* subject, a female graduate student in psychology, was used. The subject was accompanied on her ordinary daily routine on several different days by an experimenter, who interrupted her at irregular intervals to ask her what she was looking at. She then had to estimate the size of the object, the size of its retinal projection for her, and its distance from her, in two different "attitudes": "naive-perceptual" and "rationale-

---

[44] *Ibid.*, p. 131.

[45] *Ibid.*, p. 134.

[46] E. Brunswik, *The conceptual framework of psychology*. Chicago: University of Chicago Press, 1952.

betting." The experimenter, doubling as "control subject" also made estimates of the object selected by the subject; then he made actual physical measurements of the object and its distance from the subject's positions. The measured size of the objects and their mathematically calculated retinal projections were then correlated with the subject's various estimates, to show that size constancy (i.e., accuracy of size estimates) does not depend only on size of actual retinal projection, but that additional cues are used, and result in greater accuracy than retinal projection alone can account for. Notice the representative sample of stimuli, the gathering of data in the natural setting with all natural cues available, the passive role of the experimenter, and the correlational analysis.[47]

Brunswik's "representative design" raises almost insurmountable problems for person perception studies. Suppose we wanted to conduct an experiment in which we were to study an individual's ability to perceive Others' trustworthiness. Can you imagine what a sample of the perceiver's natural habitat would involve — cab drivers, retail sellers, lovers, mothers, teachers, information givers, deliverers of packages, etc. How would you establish a criterion of trustworthiness? And yet, just because a technique may be difficult, does this mean that it is undesirable?

Postman[48] has pointed out that representative design must pay its price also. Representative design has difficulty in dealing with representative states of the organism. For instance, in Brunswik's view, imperfection of perceptual achievement is considered to be only the result of ambiguities in the environment and the organism's limited capacity to utilize available cues. The problem of motivation affecting the perception is considered as so much "noise." This results in a great loss of data, since the conditions under which motivation affects perceptual achievement cannot be specified.

It is also fair to point out that there may be times when the experimenter is interested in *specific* situations. For instance, classroom learning, particular instances of interpersonal bargaining, and interracial housing patterns in public housing are all specific instances of behavior which are pervasive enough to merit study in their own right. It is obvious that both representative design and its opposite, systematic design, pay a price in the collection of information: systematic design, by artificially isolating and correlating variables; representative design by foregoing the measurement of the interaction of variables in specific situations. The conclusion is obvious: both are needed. And nowhere in the study of person perception is this better illustrated than in the study of traits that are of significance in interpersonal relations.

---

[47] I am indebted to Dr. Lindy Geis for this illustration.
[48] L. Postman, The probability approach and nomothetic theory. *Psychol. Rev.*, 1955, 62, 218–225.

Trait organization in person perception. Asch,[49] in a series of studies in which trait names were presented, asked subjects to describe Others who possessed these traits. Asch was able to demonstrate that when a person was given a list of qualities, such as intelligent, skillful, industrious, either warm or cold, determined, practical and cautious; the person described different personalities depending upon whether warm or cold had been inserted in that list. From these studies Asch was able to derive certain properties of the way in which traits interact in the perceptual process.

(1) Each trait possesses the property of a part in a whole. The introduction or omission of a single trait may alter the entire impression.

(2) Each quality functions as representative of the entire person.

(3) In the course of interaction between an impression already present and a particular quality, the concrete character of the latter is developed within the requirements set for it by its environment.

But, to demonstrate the *interactive* nature of impression formation through the use of traits, he also stated certain properties related to the perceiver.

(4) One strives to form an impression of the entire person. The impression tends to become complete even when the evidence is meager. It is hard not to see the person as a unit.

(5) The moment we see that two or more characteristics belong to the same person they enter into dynamic interaction. . . . If one person is intelligent and cheerful, and another intelligent and morose, the quality of intelligence ceases to be the same in the two.

Finally, his conclusion which is neither strictly a property of the perceiver nor the property of trait organization:

(6) From its inception the impression has a structure, even if rudimentary. The various characteristics do not possess the same weight. Some become central, providing the main direction; others become peripheral and dependent.[50]

This led later investigators to try to define centrality more clearly.

Research illustrations. Bruner, Shapiro, and Tagiuri demonstrated that traits when presented in isolation or combination do relate to certain stable inferences which may be made from one trait to another. In their experiment a subject is given a list of traits, at the head of which appears the words, "People who are

---

[49] S. E. Asch, Forming impressions of personality. *J. abnorm. soc. Psychol.*, 1946, 41, 258–290.

[50] S. E. Asch, *Social psychology*. New York: Prentice-Hall, 1952, Pp. 216–218.

considerate . . . very often, tend to be, may or may not be, tend not to be, seldom are . . . *aggressive, active, awkward,* etc." [51] They concluded, "in spite of the apparent complexity of the phenomenon, certain aspects of inference made from trait combinations can be predicted amazingly well from the characteristics of the inferences made from the components." [52] The implication of this finding is that if the perceiver learns that the Other person has X trait, the experimenter should be able to predict, from his knowledge of trait relations, that the perceiver will assign Y trait to the Other also. The researchers argue that this trait combination is appropriate for abstract or non-real persons, or for classes of persons such as Irish, Republicans, or slum landlords, but that it is not appropriate for the judgment of one Other individual.

To illustrate this argument, Secord, Bachman, and Eachus,[53] in dealing with fifteen different traits, demonstrated that those traits perceived to have been changed by their experimental manipulations of their subjects were also changed by the subjects when describing their best friends.

Another study by Bramel[54] was even more dramatic, because he was able to demonstrate that momentarily increasing the salience of a trait for the perceiver (in this case by leading the perceiver to believe that he had strong latent homosexual tendencies) will cause the perceiver to ascribe that trait to his best friend.

These two studies and others (Benedetti and Hill)[55] suggest that the organization of traits may be more a function of the perceiver (i.e., whether and to what degree he has the trait in question) when the perceiver is judging one Other individual who is a friend than a function of trait organization in the perceived per se. At any rate, all the studies combined emphasize once more the importance of the need to manipulate both the perceiver and the perceived when trying to understand person perception.

The Situation

In addition to the perceiver and the perceived, it was suggested earlier that the *situation* in which the perceiving is done needs to be investigated. The demand properties of the situation raise the question for the subject, "why am I forming this impression of an Other?" As has been noted in many of the studies

---

[51] J. S. Bruner, D. Shapiro & R. Tagiuri, The meaning of traits in isolation and in combination. In R. Tagiuri & L. Petrullo (Eds.), *Person perception and interpersonal behavior.* Stanford: Stanford University Press, 1958. Pp. 277–289.

[52] *Ibid.,* p. 289.

[53] P. F. Secord, C. W. Backman & H. T. Eachus, Effects of imbalance in the self concept on the perception of persons. *J. abnorm. soc. Psychol.,* 1964, 68, 442–446.

[54] D. Bramel, A dissonance theory approach to defensive projection. *J. abnorm. soc. Psychol.,* 1962, 64, 121–129.

[55] D. T. Benedetti & J. G. Hill, A determiner of the centrality of a trait in impression formation. *J. abnorm. soc. Psychol.,* 1960 60, 278–280.

reviewed thus far, the answer becomes — "because the experimenter wants me to." Another situational variant ought to be contained in the problem of what the subject thinks he is going to *do* with the impression once it is formed.

Research illustrations. Carlson[56] separated subjects into two groups which responded to the Edwards Personal Preference Scale (EPPS) and read three personality descriptions of Others composed of items related to the EPPS need scales. The situational manipulation was performed by having one group read the descriptions to choose which of the three they would "most like as a friend," while the second group read the same descriptions to choose which "would make the best leader in a social group on campus." The subjects then wrote as complete a description of each personality as they were able. One of the findings was that the number and type of recalled characteristics were positively related to the sets given to the subjects. However, these results are confounded by many of the methodological problems mentioned above, such as response set, lack of subject familiarity with the EPPS items, and contrast effects in the three descriptions.

A more convincing demonstration of situational or instructive sets upon the subject is described by Cohen.[57] Following Zajonc's[58] line of reasoning, he created two different sets of readiness. In one, "transmission tuning," the individual expects to communicate his cognitions to others; in the other, "reception tuning," the subject expects to receive additional material on the person's cognitions. Cohen's data indicate "that when actually writing their impressions, subjects respond differently to different cognitive sets. In general, subjects differ widely in whether they tend to polarize or suspend depending upon whether they are set to transmit or to receive impressions."[59] Other data show "that both in their desires for new information and in their desires for information on both sides, people set to receive Others' impressions have greater desires than people set to transmit their own impressions."[60]

In addition to instructive set, task effects have been shown to influence perception of others. Loeb, Feshbach, Beck et. al. wished to test the hypothesis with institutionalized subjects that: "High performance, relative to low performance, results in positive affect, in self-confidence, and in attribution of happiness to others."[61] Subjects were asked to judge a series of happy and sad

[56] E. R. Carlson, Motivation and set in acquiring information about persons. *J. Pers.*, 1961, 29, 285–293.

[57] A. R. Cohen, Cognitive tuning as a factor affecting impression formation. *J. Pers.*, 1961, 29, 235–245.

[58] R. B. Zajonc, The process of cognitive tuning in communication *J. abnorm. soc. Psychol.*, 1960, 61, 159–167.

[59] A. R. Cohen, *op. cit.,* p. 244.

[60] *Ibid.*, p. 245.

[61] A. Loeb, S. Feshbach, A. T. Beck & A. Wolf, Some effects of reward upon the social perception and motivation of psychiatric patients varying in depression. *J. abnorm. soc. Psychol.*, 1964, 68, 610.

faces in photos. Then, in pairs, they participated in a task which artificially produced superior individual performers. Upon completion of the task they again rated the photographs. The "superior performance subjects rate the happy stimuli as happier than they did previously and their judgments are consistently higher than those for the inferior performers." [62] However, the attribution process is seen to be equally dependent upon characteristics of the stimulus, in that the projections of positive affect occurred only in response to the happy faces. The authors, following the study made by Holmes and Berkowitz[63] also expected contrast effects, but none occurred.

Berlew and Williams[64] offer more evidence that manipulation of the situation can create differences in social perception. Their experiment essentially demonstrated that there was a negative relationship between achievement and achievement sensitivity, when subjects participated in a group discussion with the persons they were later asked to judge, and when subjects viewed those they were going to judge from behind a one-way mirror. However, their accuracy criterion is questionable. It consists of self rankings compared to others' rankings on the same dependent variable. Scoring problems aside, there is every reason to suspect that self ranking would be just as susceptible to the influence of the independent variable as is the ranking of others. The authors do raise a difficult problem in the measurement of motivation in person perception studies. They note, "Interpersonal sensitivity, like imagination, is apparently very sensitive to changes in need state, and need state, in turn, is affected by many factors which in human subjects an investigator cannot control." [65]

Summary: The Perceiver, The Perceived and The Situation

In completing the review of person perception studies which place particular emphasis on one aspect of the perceiver, the perceived or the situation, we can make the following generalizations.

Measurement problems in person perception are intense and widespread. The relative effects of the perceiver, the perceived and the situation were never adequately controlled in the studies reviewed. Most of the studies reviewed create an artificial sensitivity to the *process* of forming an impression regarding an Other rather than developing situations in which the impression formed is incidental to the activity, as is true in real life.

Too few studies reviewed made any attempt to see if the categories utilized in the act of forming an impression were meaningful to the subject. Often the

---

[62] *Ibid.*, p. 613.

[63] D. S. Holmes & L. Berkowitz, Some contrast effects in social perception. *J. abnorm. soc. Psychol.*, 1961, 62, 150—153.

[64] D. E. Berlew & A. F. Williams, Interpersonal sensitivity under motive arousing conditions. *J. abnorm. soc. Psychol.*, 1964, 68, 150—160.

[65] *Ibid.*, p. 159.

activity involving the subject was unrelated to the judgments he was asked to make.

Until recently (Hastorf, Richardson, and Dornbusch),[66] no one has attempted to discover salient categories the perceiver, if unhampered by the psychologist's paper and pencil tests, might use in forming an impression of an Other.

More person perception studies must be designed which can interdependently assess the relative contributions of the perceiver, the perceived and the situation. This is, of course, a request for more designs utilizing analysis of variance and factorial models.

One of the implications of this review is that more attention must be paid to studies in which the perceiver interacts with the perceived. More designs should be created in which accuracy is not studied for accuracy's sake, but rather for its behavioral consequences. In fact, the problem of perception and its behavioral consequences must be further studied. This leads to inspection of person perecption experiments which study interpersonal attraction and interactions between the perceiver and the stimulus person.

ASSUMED SIMILARITY AND INTERPERSONAL ATTRACTION

In the conclusion of the section on person perception and accuracy, (p. 10) it was suggested that a more fruitful mode of research might be to observe the behavioral implications which attend a particular perception. Some studies of assumed similarity to a perceived Other have done this. The purpose of this section is not to review the entire range of studies dealing with assumed similarity, but rather to select those which have shown important behavioral implications.

The assumption that an Other is similar to oneself could have many behavioral implications. One might, assuming someone else is like him, predict that the Other will act as he might in a particular situation. Thus, I might predict that my friend who is similar to me will respond to someone else's attempt to control him just as I might — or that he will respond to aggression, affection, or indifference in much the same manner as I. Thus assuming similarity or dissimilarity, in the naive psychology of the layman, may be a way of predicting behavior.

The assumption of similarity (his skin is like mine) or dissimilarity (his skin is unlike mine) when applied to groups may be basic to discriminatory behavior. Discrimination also involves generalizing from one aspect, such as skin color, to the total person. But then the assumption of similarity is, by the fact that it is an assumption, always a generalization based on partial data.

Finally, depending upon how comfortable a person feels with himself,

---

[66] A. H. Hastorf, S. A. Richardson & S. M. Dornbush, op. cit., pp. 54–63.

assuming someone else is similar may lead to attraction for that person, increased interaction, etc.

Research illustrations. At one time Byrne[67] believed that the effect of attitude similarity is a sufficient cause for liking someone. He conducted an experiment in which subjects were led to believe that some strangers held attitudes similar to their own, while others held dissimilar attitudes. His results indicated significantly more positive feelings toward the "stranger" who was believed to hold similar attitudes than toward the dissimilar stranger. Once more the similar stranger was judged to be more intelligent, better informed, more moral, and better adjusted than the stranger with dissimilar attitudes.

But the problem of causation is not as simple and straightforward as Byrne's early study might indicate. Backman and Secord[68] argue, "that persons who are attracted to other persons on some grounds other than similarity tend to perceive such others as attracted to them." [69] Thus, they suggest that cause and effect might work either way: "If one likes another person, he perceives the other as liking him; or (b) if one perceives another as liking him, he is likely to be attracted to the other." [70] Backman and Secord induced similarity by telling the subjects that certain others with whom they were going to interact liked them. Then, sociometric data were collected over six group discussion sessions of the individuals. The data reveal that the persons whom the subject believed they were liked by were chosen significantly more often in the first session, but not more often in the remaining sessions. This introduction of the time element suggests that having information about an Other prior to interaction may, in fact, lead to initial attraction, but that the behavioral data generated through interaction may change this. Thus, the relation of assumed similarity to interpersonal attraction may be a temporary one.

The most informative study of interpersonal attraction and assumed similarity over time is that of Newcomb.[71] Newcomb was able to observe interpersonal attraction of two 17-man populations over a four-month period in a natural setting. College students coming to the university were recruited to live together and to participate in the study for their board. Newcomb employed Heider's balance theory to help him to understand interpersonal attraction in this setting. Newcomb comments, "for the purpose of this study, the elements among which a balanced relationship may exist for an individual are: his degree of attraction, positive or negative, toward another individual; his attitude,

---

[67] D. Byrne, Interpersonal attraction and attitude similarity. *J. abnorm. soc. Psychol.*, 1961, 62, 713–715.

[68] C. W. Backman & P. F. Secord, The effect of perceived linking on interpersonal attraction, *Human Relations*, 1959, 12, 379–385.

[69] *Ibid.*, p. 379.

[70] *Ibid.*

[71] T. M. Newcomb, Stabilities underlying changes interpersonal attraction. *J. abnorm. soc. Psychol.*, 1963, 66, 376–386.

favorable or unfavorable, toward some object, and the second individual's attitude, as perceived by the first individual, toward the same object." [72] Newcomb is able to show that the various elements mentioned above became stable at different rates over the fifteen week period. For instance, perceptions of own and Other's attitudes toward self or objects might vary radically over the period of time investigated. But, "with regard to such diverse attitude objects as the individual subject himself, other group members, and a range of non-person objects, such a relationship, described as a balanced one, is found at all stages of acquaintance. This constant relationship is maintained despite the fact that all of the related elements are changing, or some of them are changing while others are not." [73]

This finding again attests to the fact that assumed similarity is a rather temporary condition which may or may not be confirmed by interaction – all of which suggests that *liking* is a function of veridical reciprocal interactive reward systems, and may be only initially and quite momentarily explained by the assumption of similarity. However, this argument assumes that when a perceiver is confronted with behavioral data which conflict with his perception, he will modify the perception rather than "explain away" or deny the behavioral data. The data indicate that this assumption doesn't always hold true.

For instance, Newcomb, in reporting the above study more thoroughly, discovered individual differences in the way authoritarians and non-authoritarians dealt with discrepancies between attraction and assumed similarity. He reports:

> In ways that differ with the stage of acquaintance and with the nature of objects of orientation, non-authoritarians appear to be particularly sensitive to matters of strain and balance. With increasing opportunity for obtaining information about their fellows, they tend, more than authoritarians, to become more accurate in estimating their fellows' orientations. At early stages of acquaintance, however, their sensitivity to balance may – if the objects of orientation are of sufficiently great importance – outweigh their tendency toward accuracy, in an autistic manner. . . . The authoritarians, contrastingly, tended to continue to perceive more agreement than actually existed with those whom they were already attracted to.[74]

Tying perception of others to extended behavioral situations, as Newcomb has done, has two very important implications for the type of accuracy studies reviewed earlier. First, that accuracy may change over time and may differentially change for individuals, and second, that *inaccuracy* may actually serve

---

[72] *Ibid.*, p. 385.

[73] *Ibid.*

[74] T. M. Newcomb, *The acquaintance process.* New York: Holt, Rinehart & Winston, 1961. p. 143.

the interests of some individuals as they go about organizing their perceptual world. For instance, Byrne and Blaylock found that in married couples, "for both sexes, there is a strong tendency to distort modest actual similarities in the direction of much greater congruence than is objectively present." [75]

Summary. These studies of assumed similarity, while making important contributions methodologically (in the sense that the investigators have usually been able to demonstrate that the perceptual act of assuming similarity will have behavioral implications), still suffer from some of the same inadequacies of the earlier accuracy studies. The concept of assumed similarity is too broad. For instance, do the results discussed hold equally well when the perceiver assumes similarity on the basis of dimensions which are *salient* for him, as when he assumes similarity on the basis of dimensions which are not salient, or are irrelevant? Would the reaction to a disconfirmation of assumed similarity be the same for salient and irrelevant dimensions?

Finally, in all the studies reviewed, and others read but not reviewed, the *experimenter* has been the one who selects the dimensions along which judgments of assumed similarity are formed. This leaves untouched the question of whether a perceiver, left to select dimensions within a range of possible dimensions, would select dimensions which were salient for him in assuming similarity. It also leaves unanswered — and even unquestioned — whether individual salience would be simply a function of the situation and thus salient for all individuals in the situation; or whether salience is different for each individual, or a function of both the situation and individual differences. These questions will be explored further in the experiment designed for this study.

INTERACTION AND PERSON PERCEPTION

The evaluative stimulus person. Person perception studies become truly interactive when the subject not only makes a judgment about an Other, but also is allowed to relate actively to a stimulus person. For instance, Jones, Gergen, and Davis[76] had two groups of forty females interviewed by an interviewer who indicated his positive or negative reactions to each female. The two groups of girls were divided according to their scores on Christie's Mach Scales. The principal findings were: (a) the subjects' impressions of a disapproving source were far more negative in tone than those formed of an approving source; (b) Machiavellianism had no effect on the subject's impression of the interviewers; and (c) different patterns of reaction in self-presentation occurred

[75] D. Byrne & B. Blaylock, Similarity and assumed similarity of attitudes between husbands and wives. *J. abnorm. soc. Psychol.*, 1963, 67, 639.

[76] K. J. Gergen, E. E. Jones & K. E. Davis, Some determinants of reactions to being approved or disapproved as a person. *Psychol. Monogr.*, 1962, 76, (2, Whole No. 521), 1–17.

depending upon where the subjects stood on the Mach Scales, with lows being more responsive to variations in feedback. A very interesting finding was that the personality disposition did not affect description of the Other, but was related to variations in impressions of self.

Iverson[77] has carried evaluation of the stimulus person even one step further by ascribing status to the evaluator. In two experiments, subjects listened to speeches by persons who were either of high or low status and who delivered either self-punitive, extra-punitive, or non-punitive speeches. The findings indicate that it is all right for high status persons to punish the audience by verbal redress. "Observers who were the target of extra-punitive remarks did not seem to be offended, but instead seemed to regard such criticism from superiors as an appropriate form of role behavior, for example, arousing others to perform socially desired deeds." [78] In fact, according to Iverson's findings, it is also all right for high status persons to be self-punitive – this makes him more "humane." But when a low status person exhibited the same sort of behavior, he was described as being "burdensome" to listeners and as "hypocritical" and "hostile" in manner.

> Results of both studies pointed, however, to certain limiting conditions with regard to the subjects' deferential treatment of high status persons. In Experiment I when superior ranking speakers castigated themselves but not their audience, they appeared to arouse ambivalence in perceivers, i.e., they displayed behavior with low-power implications which was perceived as incongruent with their high ascribed power value. . . . when self-punitive stimulus persons attempted to involve observers in a positive way, namely, by praising them, then observer's personality impressions tended to undergo general reorganization. Superior personages in condemning self but in praising rather than reproving others aroused a generally unfavorable reaction in perceivers.[79]

So it seems that the stimulus person can change the perceiver's impression of him, either by directly devaluating the perceiver, or by exhibiting properties which seem incongruent with the perceiver's understanding of the stimulus person's status and power. Both findings add support to the contention that more attention needs to be paid to interaction between the stimulus person and the perceiver in the person perception experiment.

Interactive design. Allowing the perceiver to interact with the perceived increases the complexity of trying to sort out the effects of the perceiver from those of the perceived exponentially. Criterion problems are no longer only related to the perceiver or the perceived, but rather are a function of the

---

[77] M. A. Iverson, Personality impressions of punitive stimulus persons of differential status. *J. abnorm. soc. Psychol.*, 1964, 68, 617–626.

[78] *Ibid.*, p. 624.

[79] *Ibid.*, p., 617–626.

perceiver, the perceived, *and* the situation. The inadequacies of the studies reviewed so far have increasingly pointed toward the conclusion that research designs in person perception must reflect this complexity. It has been suggested that an adequate design must assess the variance in results due to: (1) relevent properties of the perceiver; (2) variations in the stimulus person; and (3) differences in situational elements. This assumes that it is the relationship among the above three that will promote knowledge more effectively than examination of individual elements alone. Such a design has been developed by Bernard Pyron.[80]

First, Pyron discusses what he has decided will be the relevant aspects of the perceiver. The variable he discusses is the perceiver's propensity for using a rather limited range of dimensions in forming an impression of an Other. Next, he considers the stimulus person, but in *relation* to the perceiver. Thus, he hypothesizes that perceivers use a limited number of dimensions, and tend not to make use of the concrete data of the Other's actions at a given time and in a given situation. This leads Pyron to the expectation that if the "Others whose behavior (to be predicted) could easily be ordered along a single dimension, (the Other) would be predicted more accurately than Others whose behavior could not be ordered along a single dimension."[81] Thus Pyron develops two general types of Others, one globally consistent and one not. In the experiment, the Other is manipulated so that he will be globally consistent *across* "four different types of situations: ethical; religious; interpersonal situations, not involving ethical codes; and situations involving the choice of musical selection."[82] In addition, the Other is arranged so that he will be consistent or inconsistent *within* each of the above situations. Thus, there are two kinds of consistency: "the consistency with a single, global dimension across situational types (global consistency); and consistency within situational types (situational consistency)."[83]

In an improvement over the studies reviewed, the perceivers in this study knew what the choice of the Other was, following each of 48 predictions, "and curves relating accuracy to blocks of predictions were constructed."[84]

Pyron designs two types of consistency: the consistency of a single, global dimension across such situations as ethical, religious, interpersonal situations not involving ethical codes, and situations involving the choice of musical selection. Such consistency is illustrated (according to the author) in the individual who is ethical, conventionally religious, submissive in interpersonal situations, and likes popular music (the consistent conformist). Pyron predicts that the behavior of

---

[80] Bernard Pyron, Accuracy of interpersonal perception as a function of consistency of information. *J. Pers. soc. Psychol.*, 1965, 1, 111–118.

[81] *Ibid.* p. 111.

[82] *Ibid.*, p. 112.

[83] *Ibid.*

[84] *Ibid.*

such a globally consistent individual would be more easily predicted by a subject than an Other who is ethical, not religious, not submissive in interpersonal situations, but prefers popular music.

Pyron's design is constructed so that within each of the four situations described above there are twelve sub-situations involving choice behavior of the Other. The Other is also manipulated to be consistent or inconsistent in these sub-situations; this Pyron calls situation consistency. For example, an Other who is submissive toward all others is situationally consistent; whereas, an Other who is submissive toward parents and peers, but not teachers, is situationally inconsistent.

The task of the subject is to predict the Other's choice in each of the sub-situations and across the four situations. The subjects were told what the Other's choice was at the end of each sub-situation. In introducing each of the four major situations, the subject is told what the Other's first choice is, which is intended to create the sets of ethical, religious, interpersonal, and type of music preferred.

The predicting sequence was divided into blocks of trials so that there are six blocks and eight predictions within each block. The total design thus fits a 2 by 2 by 2 by 6 repeated measures analysis of variance.

The author does not discuss what evidence he has that the manipulations of global consistency and situation consistency were effective. This represents a serious shortcoming in the journal article (the article is a condensed version of a Ph. D. thesis, and perhaps the manipulations are discussed in the original work). Certain of the results described were made equivocal by a lack of clarity as to whether (a) the ethical, religious, interpersonal, and musical situations really allowed the subject to see those situations as consistent or inconsistent or (b) whether the subject saw the resolutions of the situations as being consistent or inconsistent for the *individual.* For instance, Pyron reports that, "for the global consistent conditions, the nonconformist was predicted more accurately than the conformist." [85] Pyron had predicted that accuracy would increase for both the conformist and the nonconformist. He does not attempt to explain the results he obtained. Once more, in introducing the study he suggests "that Others whose behavior (to be predicted) could easily be ordered along a single dimension would be predicted more accurately than Others whose behavior could not." [86]

Similarly, another puzzling finding is that the analysis of variance shows "that the effects of global consistency occur only for the situation consistent conditions." [87] Pyron does attempt to explain this as simply being an artifact of the fact that situation consistency accounts for so much of the variance.

---

[85] *Ibid.*, p. 115.
[86] *Ibid.*, p. 111.
[87] *Ibid.*, p. 115.

28

However, alternative explanations might justifiably be offered, such as the ones suggested earlier: the manipulation of global consistency is not working, or the perceiver may be attending to the situation more than to the global consistency of the Other.

Pyron also developed a measure of the effect of assumed similarity between the judge and the Other which resulted in his conclusion that "the greater the ambiguity, the greater is the tendency of the judge to rely upon his own position in predicting the Other, and the greater is his inability to differentiate the Other from himself." [88] The main problem with the design is that the complexity of the manipulations tends to confound the complexity of the relationships discovered among the perceiver, perceived, and the situation.

All in all, it is an ambitious and well thought through design. It rightfully calls into question the designs reviewed earlier which concentrate so heavily on *only* one of the elements, such as the perceiver, in person perception. (It is interesting to note that Pyron[89] found extremely small perceiver effects in this study.)

---

[88] *Ibid.*, p. 117.
[89] *Ibid.*, p. 115.

II

The Theoretical and Experimental Context

A THEORETICAL ORIENTATION

It should be obvious by now that just as studies which emphasize one aspect of the person perception situation prove inadequate in the long run, any theory which has as its focus single elements will also be inadequate for understanding person perception.

Deutsch and Krauss[1] have argued that constructs within a theory which can not show multiple connection to other constructs or observable events are of little use. A similar argument has been developed here concerning experimentation in person perception. What good is it to perseverate on interpersonal accuracy, unless accuracy can be shown to be related to behavior? As long as interpersonal accuracy is operationally defined as one person matching another's response to MMPI items or an adjective check list, little knowledge is gained, since accuracy is specific to the measure used and it is not clear what rule of correspondence would tie the measure to observable behavior. No matter how many different ways accuracy is operationally defined, until it is related to other constructs or behavior one can never be sure that the measurement of "interpersonal accuracy" will help in understanding the act of perceiving another person.

The argument of multiple connection can also be used as a criterion in searching for a theory which will aid in the understanding of person perception. That is, the theory should be able to account for the *relations* among the attributes of the perceiver, the perceived, and the situation. Historically, the social psychological theories which have done this best have been those of the Gestaltists. Consider the major notion of Gestalt theory described by Deutsch and Krauss, ". . . psychological phenomena should be conceived as occurring in a 'field' — as part of a system of co-existing and mutually interdependent factors

---

[1] M. Deutsch & R. Krauss, *Theories in social psychology*,1965. New York: Basic Books Inc., p. 8.

having certain properties as a system that are not deducible from knowledge of the isolated elements of the system." [2]

The implication of this notion for person perception seems to be clear. Psychological phenomena such as "differential accuracy," "stereotype accuracy," considered apart from their interdependence with the "fields" or situations in which they are studied, will not lead to understandings of the total act of person perception.

Illustration of this notion is found in the following discussion by Newcomb. Building on the thought of Cassirer that, "throughout the history of mathematics and physics, problems of constancy of relations rather than of constancy of elements have gained importance and have gradually changed the picture of what is essential," [3] Newcomb reports constancies of relations among varying cognitions of attitudes toward Others, objects, and Other's attitudes toward the objects. Without invoking a principle which would suggest the nature of the relationship among the cognitions (in this case the notion of balance), Newcomb's findings would have been unintelligible. [4]

There is a need in thinking about person perception to look for such principles. In the present study, such a principle is being invoked in the form of the major hypothesis. The hypothesis states that:

> In forming an impression of an Other, the perceiver will seek information that is a function of its *salience* to the perceiver and its *relevance* to the situation in which the impression is formed.

This is intended to be an hypothesis in the Gestalt tradition which brings together elements of the person — the salience of the information to him — with elements of the situation — the relevance of the information to the situation — into a relationship which is a better predictor of behavior than a consideration of either salience or relevance independently would yield.

This major hypothesis is not unrelated to other theories or research. Heider, in describing the perceptual process, said: "Obviously, the existence of the other person, O, as an object with not only physical and spatial particulars, but also with complex psychological properties, must be mediated in some way to the subject, that is, perceived by P, if O is to feature in P's thinking, feelings, and actions." [5] For Heider, the causal "cores," such as intention and ability attributed to the perceived by the perceiver, become the foci for his discussion rather than the mediation process.

---

[2] *Ibid.*, p. 16.

[3] E. Cassirer, *Substance and function*. Chicago: Open Court, 1923, p. 5.

[4] T. M. Newcomb, Stabilities underlying changes in interpersonal attraction. *J. abnorm. soc. Psychol.*, 1963, 66, (4) p. 385.

[5] F. Heider, *The psychology of interpersonal relations*. New York: John Wiley, 1958, p. 20.

In the present study, however, the mediation process is of more interest. It is suggested that in forming an impression of an Other, the impression will be mediated by the available information's salience and relevance. Salience and relevance act as a set of interdependent weights which will affect what is attended to by the perceiver.

That a system of weights mediates and organizes our impressions is not a new idea. Newcomb states, "We judge people in terms of their attitudes, to be sure, but not indiscriminately; we *weigh* some kinds of attitudes heavily in *whatever scales we use*, while regarding others as minor, or even ignoring them. They are weighed, somehow, in terms of our own attitudes as cognizers" [6] [italics added]. Newcomb assumes that perceivers have habits of attributing their own attitudes to similar Others.

The hypothesis in this paper suggests that the perceiver habitually attends to information which is salient and relevant in the universe of perceptual information available.

It should be noted that forming an impression is a momentary process. Therefore, the phenomena covered by the hypothesis stated above are short-lived. However, the impression formed will have implications for further perception; it will lead to such attributions as assumed similarity, interpersonal attraction, intentions, and causality. It will affect the more durable mediation processes described by Heider. For if, in our perceptions of Others, we attend to that which is salient for us and relevant to the situation and in so doing learn where the Other stands in relation to the information to which we are attending, then we might expect that our next perceptual act will be to evaluate the person being perceived. A great deal of literature, both theoretical and experimental, exists to support the notion that we do evaluate others in perceiving them. Among the general propositions that have wide acceptance in social psychology are those which focus on the observed correlations among *feelings of positive affect, social acts of comparison,* and the *perception of similarity* between persons.

Boring[7] suggests that "as long as a new construct has only the single operational definition that it received at birth, it is just a construct." I am suggesting that as long as an hypothesis has implications only for the experiment designed to test it, then it is only a tribute to operationism and not to knowledge. To prevent operationism, considerable effort is made to connect the impression formation hypothesis stated here to theoretical propositions dealing with assumed similarity, feelings of positive affect and social comparison.

---

[6] T. M. Newcomb, The cognition of persons as cognizers. In R. Tagiuri & L. Pertrullo (Eds.), *Person perception and interpersonal behavior.* Stanford, Stanford University Press, 1958, p. 180.
[7] E. G. Boring, *History, psychology, and science; selected papers.* New York: John Wiley, 1963, p. 222.

THE EXPERIMENTAL CONTEXT

Just as it was important to formulate an hypothesis which could simultaneously account for relationships among the various aspects of a person perceiving an Other and at the same time be responsive to the need for an interactive experiment in person perception, it is also important to discover a context in which the hypothesis might best be tested. The criteria for such a context seem fairly evident. First, some property of the person must be selected which is either conceptually or experimentally of potential importance for perception. Next, the stimulus person being described must be capable of being defined and manipulated under experimental conditions. The situation must be one in which the outcomes are clear and controllable. Finally, the variance contributed by the perceiver, the perceived, and the situation should be measurable and separable analytically.

The person property. The first property of the perceiver which was suggested by previous literature was that of authoritarianism. But authoritarianism was rejected for two reasons: first, because of Newcomb's[8] adequate exploration of the way authoritarians perceive others over time; second, because of the conviction that authoritarianism is beginning to "show its age." That is, there is some doubt whether the political structures and attitudes underlying its original conceptualization are appropriate for our times.

The personality disposition finally arrived at is that of Machiavellianism. Basic to the idea of Machiavellianism (as it is used in this work) is the tendency to view Others as impersonal objects and as objects for manipulation rather than as persons. Given the formulations by Heider and Newcomb reviewed earlier which suggested that basically different processes were involved in perceiving objects and in perceiving persons, there is an implication that the Machiavellian's perceptual processes may be different from those of a person who takes a more humanitarian view towards others.

The stimulus person. Two theoretical stimulus persons were constructed for this study using Q-sort items which had been judged relevent to Machiavellianism. The items provided a coherent "Other" both theoretically and by the subject's actual observation. These items formed the basic information upon which the subject was to form an impression. The ten statements relevant to Machiavellianism were embedded in the thirty-six statements of Table 3 (p. 52). When the subjects were to receive an impression that the Other was competitive (i.e., high Machiavellian) they "learned" that the "Other" had sorted a statement such as "I value power for myself and in others" as being very characteristic. When the "Other" was to be seen as cooperative (i.e., low Machiavellian) the subjects "learned" that the above statement was *un*characteristic of the Other.

---

[8] T. M. Newcomb, Stabilities underlying changes in interpersonal attraction, pp. 376–386.

The situation. The situation selected for the enactment of this person perception study is that of interpersonal bargaining. Interpersonal bargaining is viewed here as an instance of social interaction amenable to analysis within the framework of person perception. This is in keeping with the analysis of bargaining presented by Deutsch and Krauss.[9] For purposes of this study, one of the most important aspects of the bargaining situation is the interdependence it creates between the bargainers. Knowing that you are about to enter into an interdependent relationship with another person should provide a reason for forming an impression of that other person. For instance, bargainers usually want to know if the other can be trusted, if he is aggressive, naive, etc.

Interpersonal bargaining, in a game format, also permits easy assessment of the role of the bargainer's own orientation, his expectation of how the Other will bargain, and the interaction between bargainers. In this experiment, the use of the interpersonal bargaining game also permits one to discover what the behavioral implications are of having formed an impression in a specified context. The game selected, which will be described later, was developed by Hornstein and Deutsch.[10]

THE EXPERIMENT

Purpose

There are three major purposes in this experiment; first, to create a design which is responsive to the inadequacies described in the preceding review of research on person perception. For instance, the experiment is designed to: (1) study simultaneously the role of the perceiver, the perceived, and the situation (2) allow the perceiver to select dimensions which are important to him in forming an impression and (3) provide an opportunity for the perceiver to act on his impression. In so doing, this experiment should demonstrate that a more adequate methodology is available to study impression formation in person perception.

Second, the design enables a test of the hypothesis:

In forming an impression of an Other, the perceiver will seek information that is a function of its *salience* to the perceiver and its *relevance* to the situation in which the impression is formed

This hypothesis embodies a Field Theoretical point of view which claims that by focusing on the coexistence and interdependence of phenomena more knowledge is produced than is obtainable from a study of the isolated elements.

[9] M. Deutsch & R. Krauss, Studies of interpersonal bargaining. *J. Confl. Resol.*, 1962, 6, 52–76.
[10] H. A. Hornstein & M. Deutsch, *The tendencies to compete and to attack as a function of inspection, incentive, and available alternatives.* (Mimeo.), 1965.

Third, it is hoped that the design will prove to be heuristic. It is intended to raise some questions about the role of one's own personality orientation and one's perception of the Other in an interpersonal bargaining situation that have not been considered by research designs in either person perception or interpersonal bargaining.

Overview of Design

The basic design (see Table 1) employed the technique of splitting 80 subjects into high and low Machiavellians. Each of these two sets of subjects was again split into two groups under different impression formation conditions. In the first impression condition, 40 subjects were given information designed to induce a perception of the stimulus person (the Other) as possessing characteristics of a *high* Machiavellian. In the second condition 40 subjects were induced to view the stimulus person as a *low* Machiavellian. It was assumed that the high Mach would appear competitive and the low cooperative. The subjects then played an interpersonal bargaining game against a programmed Other who was programmed in such a way as to either confirm or disconfirm the subjects' expectations.

Subjects

The 80 subjects were drawn from a large subject pool processed through the social psychology laboratory. The only restrictions placed upon the subjects were that they be at least seventeen years of age and male. This resulted in a relatively heterogeneous sample, in terms of the setting from which they came. The settings included: a vocational high school, three undergraduate colleges, three different divisions of two different graduate schools, and a professional organization. The subjects' ages ranged from seventeen to fifty-nine with a mean age of twenty-nine. (See Appendix XIII.)

Each High Mach and each Low Mach was routinely assigned to one of four basic conditions described in Table 1. The Mach score was known by the experimenter for the first 30 subjects during the experiment, for the rest their Mach score was not known and they were assigned to the conditions by persons other than the experimenter.[11]

Before following the procedures in detail it is important to be familiar with the entire experiment. Therefore, an overall description of each task each subject performed precedes a presentation of the procedures in depth.

---

[11] Internal analyses were conducted by an independent researcher who looked for differences between subjects run early in the experiment and those run later. Also, the researcher looked for differences between those whose Mach scores were known and those whose scores were not. No differences were found. (See Appendix XI.)

Table 1

Design Format

High Mach (N = 40)				Low Mach (N = 40)			
Forms impression of Other who is Cooperative-Low (N = 20)		Forms impression of Other who is Competitive-High (N = 20)		Forms impression of Other who is Cooperative-Low (N = 20)		Forms impression of Other who is Competitive-High (N = 20)	
Expectation Disconfirmed (N = 10)	Expectation Confirmed (N = 10)	Expectation Disconfirmed (N = 10)	Expectation Confirmed (N = 10)	Expectation Disconfirmed (N = 10)	Expectation Confirmed (N = 10)	Expectation Disconfirmed (N = 10)	Expectation Confirmed (N = 10)

Design Outline

Task one. The subject completes Mach Scales IV and V. (See Appendixes I and II.)

Task two. The subject completes a thirty-six statement Q sort. (The instructions for sorting are in Appendix III and the statements in Table 3, p. 51.)

Task three. The subject plays 35 rounds of a 70-round interpersonal bargaining game. In this game the subject can produce individualistic, cooperative, competitive, or defensive products. The payoffs for the products are designed to allow the subject's own tendencies to compete or cooperate determine his bargaining behavior.

Tasks four and five. The subject is given the opportunity to learn what a new "Other" bargainer is going to be like by selecting statements supposedly from the "Other's" Q sort. Half of the subjects are given information which makes the "Other" look competitive and half are given information which makes the "Other" look cooperative.

The subject records his impression of the Other on a semantic differential instrument (see Appendix VII) and estimates what percent of the time the Other will play individually, cooperatively, and competitively.

Task six. The subject plays the last thirty-five rounds of the bargaining game; supposedly with the person he has just formed an impression of. For half of the subjects, the expectation of how the Other will play is confirmed. The remaining subjects receive a disconfirmation of their expectation.

Task seven: the third impression. Following the completion of the bargaining game, the subject again records his impression of the Other.

Procedures

Task one: subject completes Mach scales. As the subject comes into the lab, he is directed to a small room equipped with a one-way screen and a communication system. He is told to sit at a table and that instructions for the entire study will be given to him over the public address system. On the table in front of the subject are the various instruments and papers he will need for the experiment. He is allowed to sit in the room for at least five minutes before the experiment begins. At the end of five minutes he hears the following taped instructions over the public address system:

"It looks like we are all here now, so allow me to tell you how the persons in this study are arranged. You are each sitting in a small room which can be viewed from where I am sitting in the central control room. It is possible for me or my assistant to speak to each of you individually. We can see you through the one-way mirror in your rooms. If at any point you have any questions, just raise your hand and we will talk with you over the public address system. You will not be able to see or hear each other so any questions that you ask will be repeated so that each of you will hear each question. Most of the instructions you will receive have been tape recorded — in fact, what you are now hearing has been recorded. They are recorded so that they will be the same each time they are used. But it is possible to stop the tape at any time if you have any questions.

"First of all, look at the little card which has your number on it. Now will person number one please raise your hand so that I can see you know your number." (Tape stops and the experimenter says, "All right, and can you hear well enough?") "Now person number two will you do the same." (Tape stops and the experimenter repeats question asked of number one. Recall that person number two is fake.)

The tape continues: "Now we are ready to begin. This is a study of personality and decision making. It involves six tasks. In the first task you are to complete the first two inventories which are lying on the table in front of you. They are entitled 'Opinion Inventory and Mach V Attitude Inventory.' The directions are contained on the first page of each, but if you have any questions just raise your hand. When you are finished, they will be picked up." (For a complete description of the development of the Mach Scales see Appendix IX.)

Summary: task one. To this point the subject has been given a basic induction that there are others in the experiment; he has learned to talk with the experimenter over the public address system and has completed the Mach Scales.

Task two: the Q sort. After the subject has completed the Mach Scales, two minutes have elapsed, and the inventories have been picked up. The tape begins:

"Now that all of you have completed the inventories let us begin this second task. On the table you will find a pack of three by five cards. The directions for sorting these cards are contained on the white sheet in front of you entitled 'Instructions for Card Sorting.' Again if you have any questions, just raise your hand." (For instructions see Appendix III.)

The purpose of the Q sort is to permit the experimenter to determine which statements are salient for the subject and to provide the subject with a source of meaningful information with which he can form an impression of the Other later.

When the subject finishes sorting the thirty-six items, the experimenter asks him to read off the numbers on the back of the Q-sort cards. The numbers correspond to the numbers of the statements in Table 3 on p. 52 and were recorded by the experimenter according to the pile in which they were sorted.

As soon as the statements were recorded, the subject was asked to sort through the piles once more, this time looking for the five most important and five least important statements only. For each subject, importance was described in the following example: "Suppose you had sorted the statement, 'I enjoy photography' into a pile that indicated that it was very characteristic of you. This might or might not be important to you."

When this sorting task was completed, the numbers of the ten statements were again recorded. The experimenter then said, "Person number two isn't quite finished. When he is, you will hear the instructions for the next task." A period of one minute is allowed to elapse, during which time the peg board to be used in the next task is placed in the room with the subject; another minute elapses and the tape begins again.

Task three: the bargaining game. The tape begins:

"In this third task the two number one persons will be working with the two number two persons. In other words, each of you is paired with one person. You will all receive the same instructions, but from now on I will be working with one pair while my assistant works with the other. This task involves the large peg board in front of you. This task is essentially a decision-making task. That is, each of you in each pair is going to engage in a decision-making task in which each of you should have the same objective: to earn as much as you can.

"To begin with, I am going to credit each of you with forty cents. So, at this point you each have forty cents. The nature of this is such that you can lose this forty cents or win more money depending upon the decisions you make. In this task you will be faced with the decision of producing either black products, blue products, red products or green products."

The subject has a peg board in front of him which has the above colors painted over columns of thirty-five holes. (See Diagram A.) Each of the five colors is painted twice with one set of colored columns being the resource area and the other set the production area. Inserted in the colored columns in the resource area are matching colored pegs.

"Products are produced by moving a peg of a particular color from the resource area to its appropriate place in the production area. For instance, a red product is made by moving a red peg from the red column in the resource area to the red column in the production area. This will be

	PRODUCTION AREA					RESOURCE AREA				
	Black	Blue	Red	Orange	Green	Black	Blue	Red	Orange	Green
1.	●	O	O	O	O	O	●	●	●	●
2.	O	O	O	O	O	●	●	●	●	●
3.	O	O	O	O	O	●	●	●	●	●
4.	O	O	O	O	O	●	●	●	●	●
5.	O	O	O	O	O	●	●	●	●	●
6.	O	O	O	O	O	●	●	●	●	●
7.	O	O	O	O	O	●	●	●	●	●
			Inspection					Inspection		
8.	O	O	O	O	O	●	●	●	●	●
70.	O	O	O	O	O	●	●	●	●	●

Diagram A. Peg Board

Explanation: The rows (numbered 1 to 70) correspond to the rounds of bargaining. The empty O's stand for the empty holes and the ●'s stand for the holes filled with pegs. The pegs and the columns are colored according to the labels at the top. In the diagram one black product has been produced thus: the "hole" in row one, black column of the resource area is empty and the "hole" in row one, black column of the production area is filled. Inspections follow every seven rounds.

Rationale: This bargaining game represents an improvement over prisoner dilemma games because it: (1) increases the number of choices available and is therefore not limited to two-signal language and (2) provides for a defensive strategy which protects the subject from a competitive Other without forcing counter-aggression.

explained in greater detail later. But just for practice, will each of you please make a red product now so that I can see that you understand how products are made. Take the red peg in row one of the resource area and move it to row one of the production area."

The tape stops and the experimenter informs person number one whether or not his move is correct. He then does likewise for the hypothetical person number two. The tape continues:

"Now will you please return the red peg.

As we go along you may have questions, but please hold them until the end of the directions and they will be answered at that time. Now, let me tell you about the different products and what they mean. Turn to the yellow sheet" (see Appendix IV) "entitled 'Summary of Product Values'. It will help you to understand the products." The tape is stopped for two minutes.

The taped instructions continue:

"If you produce black products, you will earn 3 cents for each one that you produce. Thus, each time you move a black peg from the black column of the resource area to the black column of the production area you will earn 3 cents."

"If you produce blue products, you will earn 6 cents for each one you produce – *if* and *only* if – the other person has produced a similar number of blue products. That is, for each *pair* of blue products that you and the other person produce, you will receive 6 cents, and the other person will receive 6 cents. By a pair it is meant that each of you contributes one blue product. However, if you produce a blue product and the other does not, then your blue product will be worth one cent and; of course, if the other person produces one product, and you do not, his will only be worth one cent.

"If you produce red or green products, neither one has immediate value. However, they can be used in capturing money from the other person. Let me indicate how the production of red and green products works. First, think of the red products as weapons to be used for attacking and the green products as anti-weapons or defenses against attacks. If you wanted to capture money from the other person with red products, you would have to attack him.

"Now, if you wish to attack the other person, you move an *orange* peg from the resource area to its appropriate place in the production area, and say the word, 'attack.' Decision making will then be stopped while the results of the attack are considered.

"In an attack, regardless of whether you are the attacker or the other is the attacker, each of you may either win or lose and sometimes neither of you will win or lose. If you choose to attack, in order for you to win, you must be able to destroy all the green products the other has produced. One of your red weapons can destroy one of his green defenses.

"Thus, if you attack and you have the same number of red products as he has green, you will destroy all of his defenses, but you will also use up all your weapons so that neither of you will receive payment from the other. But, if you, as attacker, have more red weapons than he has green defenses; for example, suppose you have four red products and the other person only has two green products, you will receive 6 cents from the other person for each of your reds *over* and *above* the other's greens, which in this case would be a total of 12 cents.

"Now if it happened that the person being attacked has more green products than the number of reds that the attacker has, the attacked will receive a payment of 6 cents for each green product that he has over and above the number of reds of the attacker. Thus if the attacker had only four red products and the attacked has six green products, the attacked would receive a payment of 12 cents from the attacker.

"It is especially important to note that an attack uses up all of the reds of the attacker and all of the greens of the attacked which have been produced before the time of the attack. But, an attack does not affect the attacker's greens or the other's reds. So after an attack, the attacker starts the next round with zero reds and the other person with zero greens. This is noted on your yellow sheet.

"Now let me explain how this decision-making task is actually carried out. There will be 35 rounds or decisions in this task. Each round will last 10 seconds. Before the beginning of each round, I will announce the number of that round. Your task on each round will be to select a peg of a particular color and place it in the hole of the same color in the row corresponding to the round announced. Thus, for example, if I were to say round one, and you wished to produce a black product, you would select a black peg from row one in the resource area and place it in the hole corresponding to row one in the black column in the production area. Please make the move at this time so that I can see that you understand." (Tape space: Experimenter tells "both" subjects whether they are correct or not.)

"Now supposing it is round two and you wish to produce a blue product; you would select the blue product from row one in the resource area and place it in the hole corresponding to row two in the production area blue column. Please make this blue product at this time." (Tape space while the experimenter watches for the move.)

"Please note that in taking pegs from the resource area, take the top most peg from each column. Thus, for example, if it were now round three and you wished to produce another black product, you would take the black peg in the resource area row two, and place it in the hole corresponding to row three in the production area.

"One other feature of this task is that you will each be given information about what the other has produced at the end of every seventh round. Thus, at the end of rounds 7, 14, 21, 28, and 35 you will receive information about what the other has produced. If you wish to write down what the other has produced, space is provided on the yellow sheet. This information can be extremely useful to you in helping you to decide what products to make." (Experimenter asks, "Are there any questions?")

Summary: tasks one through three. Thus far the subjects have completed the Mach Scales, the Q sort and have now heard the instructions for the bargaining task. They are now ready to begin the first thirty-five rounds of bargaining.

In the course of answering the subject's questions (if any), the experimenter acknowledges the hypothetical person number two, and then says:

"Person number two has asked if it is necessary to produce the blue products on the same round in order for them to be a pair. The answer is no. It is the total number of blues that are used to tally pairs. Thus, if one of you has produced fifteen blues at the end of the thirty-five rounds and the other has produced ten pairs, then there are ten pairs regardless of when the blues were produced. This would mean that the one producing ten blue products would receive 60 cents and the one producing fifteen would receive 60 cents for his paired blues and 5 cents for the unpaired blues. Is this clear to both of you?"

If there are no further questions, the tape counts off the rounds every ten seconds and the experimenter reports the progress of the task at the inspection points, describes the results of any attacks, and totals the winnings for both persons at the end of the thirty-five rounds. A special program was developed for the hypothetical second person; it might be called the "repentant aggressor strategy." A definite strategy was designed rather than a random one in order to increase the "reality" of the Other person and to reduce any confusion that a random strategy might create. The program opens up with an attack on the tenth round and then switches to a more cooperative blue strategy. The complete program is contained in Appendix V.

Task four: impression formation. After the subject has completed the first thirty-five rounds of bargaining and has been informed as to how much he and the other person have earned, he hears the following taped instructions:

"As noted earlier, while the two of you were involved in this production task, the other pair of persons was also completing this same task. At this point we are going to ask person number two in each pair to change places so that in a little while each of you will be involved with a new person. My assistant will show the number two persons to another room at this time."

At this point the experimenter leaves the control room and walks through the exact procedures that would be required if two persons were to change rooms. Thus, if the subject is listening, he would hear – insofar as the soundproofing would let him – doors closing and people walking around. After this has been done, the tape continues:

"Now, person number one, we are going to delay the number two persons in order to add a new phase to this study. They will each be taking a personality inventory so that each of you can be involved in this new phase. In this new phase we are interested in your production behavior when you have an advantage over the other person. Your advantage will be that you will know what the other person is like."

"Turn to the pink sheet on your table. On it you will find the same statements "(see Table III)" that you sorted into piles earlier. In order for you to know what the new person will be like, you can ask to see how the person sorted the statements. The way you do this is to select a statement from the thirty-six that you would like to see first, mark in the number one opposite the statement in the request column. Then mark in number two for the next statement and so on until you have numbered ten statements. When you have finished numbering ten statements, we will begin with the first statement you numbered since you wanted to see that first. I will tell you how the other person answered it in terms of how characteristic or uncharacteristic he thought it was of himself. You may want to refer to the earlier white sheet entitled "Instructions for Q sorting." Now, as in most cases where information is requested, the information will cost you one cent for each statement that I give you an answer for. The one cent will be deducted from the next forty cents that you will be given to start the next thirty-five rounds with. So, you may stop requesting statements whenever you want to. You do not have to buy all ten statements you numbered unless you want to, and, on the other hand, you may want to buy more than ten statements, which is also all right. When you are ready to begin, either my assistant or I will give you the answers you request. Are there any questions?"

When the subject indicates that he is ready to receive answers, he tells the experimenter that he wishes to see a particular statement. At this point, the set which indicates whether the other is High Mach-Competitive or Low Mach-Cooperative is created, by assigning Q sort pile numbers to the appropriate statements (see Appendix VI). Thus, for example, if the subject asked for statement number five – "I value power for myself and in others" – and the subject was in the high condition, the experimenter would say:

"The person you will be doing the production task with next answered that statement by sorting it into pile number nine, which means that it is extremely characteristic of him."

When the subject finishes asking for statements, he is instructed to complete a semantic differential instrument according to his impression of the other (Appendix VII.). He also completes an estimate of the other's anticipated production (Appendix VIII.).

Summary: Tasks one through four. Up to now, the subject has completed the Mach Scales, the Q sort, and the first thirty-five rounds of bargaining. In this last task he has selected information about the person he will bargain with in the next thirty-five rounds. Given the information, the subject has now completed the semantic differential and his estimate of the Other's future bargaining behavior. In the information received to this point, he may or may not have received some of the ten items designed to create the impression of the competitive or cooperative Other.

Task five: second impression formed. As soon as the instruments are complete, the experimenter says:

"All right, as we have indicated we were interested in seeing what kind of an impression you have formed, but we also want to maximize your advantage in this last thirty-five rounds. Therefore, at this time, we are going to give you, free of charge, the ten statements which the other person sorted into the extreme piles about himself."

Here the ten statements sorted by Christie[12] from the California Q sort and contained in Appendix VI were used. Following this, the subject was asked to complete the same semantic differential instrument by placing a check mark rather than an X on any item he wished to change. He also indicated any change in his estimates of the other's production by writing in new percentages.

Summary: task five. In this task the basic independent variable is introduced. The subjects are given the statements designed to create the desired competitive or cooperative sets. They are asked to complete their semantic differential description on the same form so that this impression is more a refinement or continuation of the first rather than a separate impression.

Task six: the final bargaining. Three minutes after the subject has completed the instruments a second time, the experimenter says over the public address system:

"Person number two, have you completed the personality inventory?" Space is provided for the hypothetical person to answer and then the experimenter says, "Person number one, have you completed the task?" "All right, we are ready to begin the last thirty-five rounds. Does either one of you need anything clarified?"

In this second thirty-five rounds the game is programmed to play either all red with four attacks or all blue. For those who are expecting a competitive other, the red strategy confirms their expectation, while for those expecting a cooperative other, the red strategy disconfirms their expectation. Similarly, the blue strategy confirms the expected cooperative other and disconfirms the expected competitive other.

Task seven: the third impression. When the game has been completed and the subject has learned what he has won and what the other has won, the experimenter says:

"Now that you have completed this task we are interested in seeing what kind of impression you have formed of the person you just went through these last thirty-five rounds with. Each of you has a blue

---
[12] Christie, R. Impersonal interpersonal orientations and behavior. Research Proposal. NSF, 1962.

personality description form on his table. Will you complete this? That completes the study. One of us will be in to talk with you when you have finished." (The "blue personality description form" is in Appendix VII.)

The post-experimental interview. Following the experiment, the experimenter interviewed the subject at some length. First, the subject was asked to associate freely about the experiment: what did he like or dislike, find interesting or boring? Most subjects responded by indicating how interesting they found the game and most commented about the other person's behavior. Secondly, a series of questions was asked which tried to discover whether the subject had suspected that there was really no other person. The questions included: "Did anything seem strange or unreal about this experiment?" "What did you think of this other person in the last 35 rounds?" "Didn't it seem strange to you that the other person played only one color?" Only four subjects had to be discarded for suspecting that there was no other person. Three other subjects who were not discarded said that they had some reservations about whether there was another person, but they said that they felt they *had* to play as though there were in order to maximize their payoffs. Many subjects indicated anger, disgust, or puzzlement over the way the person played in the conditions where their expectations were disconfirmed.

Sometimes if the subject's production behavior in the game seemed at all strange, he was asked a few questions about the game to determine whether he really understood it. Such questioning was very rare because in most cases it was possible to know whether the subject understood the game by the end of the 35th round. If there were any doubts at this point, the subject was discarded. Six subjects were discarded for this reason.

Finally, the subject was thoroughly informed about the experiment, including the fact that there was no Other, why it was necessary to deceive him, what the major hypothesis was, and whether the subject's data supported or rejected the hypothesis.

III

Impression Formation Results

Purpose

The primary foci of this chapter are: (1) to restate the hypothesis, describe the method developed for testing it, and present data from the results of the test; and (2) to examine the data which show whether the manipulations in the experiment were sucessful or not.

The major hypothesis is:

In forming an impression of an Other, the perceiver will seek information that is a function of its *salience* to the perceiver and its *relevance* to the situation in which the impression is formed.

Operational Definitions and Results

Salience. In this study salience is defined as the statements which the subject sorts into any of the following piles: extremely, quite, and fairly characteristic, and extremely, quite, and fairly *uncharacteristic.*

The underlying assumption is that those items which are most or least characteristic of the perceiver should provide the most meaningful information about an Other for that person and should, therefore, be chosen more frequently. This assumption found some support in the data. Disregarding the content of the statements chosen by the subject, for a moment examine the following distribution:

Table A (p. 76) shows that there is a tendency for statements to be selected from the extreme piles more than would be expected. In fact, a Chi-square goodness of fit test shows that the departure is well above the .05 level.

Relevance. In order to define relevance, 10 social psychology graduate students who were familiar with the bargaining game were asked to sort the 36 statements according to their relevance to the game. They were also asked to assign scale values to the eighteen relevant statements as follows:

45

Table 2. Scale Values for the Eighteen Most Relevant Statements

Statement Number	Scale Value	Statement Number	Scale Value
3	5.7	20	5.0
5	7.5	23	7.1
9	5.7	25	6.7
10	6.8	28	5.5
11	6.4	29	6.5
12	6.5	30	6.2
13	8.2	31	8.0
15	6.9	35	6.8
19	7.9	36	6.8

Assign a 9 to the 2 statements extremely relevant
Assign a 8 to the 3 statements very relevant
Assign a 7 to the 4 statements quite relevant
Assign a 6 to the 4 statements fairly relevant
Assign a 5 to the 5 statements somewhat relevant

The distribution of scale values for the 18 most relevant statements is contained in Table 2. (For the content of the statements see Table 3, p. 52; for all 36 scale values see Appendix XII.)

Defining salience and relevance in the manner described above creates a situation in which the relevant statements remain constant for all subjects, but the salient statements change for *each* subject. That is, the relevant statements are predetermined, but the salient statements change according to which statements are placed in the extreme Q-sort piles by each individual.

Test of the Hypothesis

At the point when the data for testing the hypothesis are collected, the subject has just completed 35 rounds of bargaining. He is told that he will continue the bargaining with a new person shortly, but that this time he will have the advantage of knowing what the other bargainer is like. In order to learn what the Other is like, he is permitted to buy, at one cent per statement, any of the 36 statements which the Other has already sorted.

The 80 subjects in this experiment bought 374 statements. Of the 374 bought, only 37 were not relevant or salient. This looks like a very significant result. However, discovering the precise probability of obtaining this result proved to be a very complex task.

At first, it appeared that the simplest test might be to categorize each statement bought into four categories: (1) relevant and salient; (2) relevant only; (3) salient only; or (4) neither relevant or salient. A Chi-square test could then be calculated between the number of statements expected to fall in each of the four categories and the actual number occuring in each category. This assumes that the probability of a statement falling into any one of the four categories is equal. However, this assumption is incorrect for the simple reason that if a subject buys five statements and the first one comes from the relevant only category then there is not an equal chance of drawing another from that category.

Other avenues of testing the hypothesis were explored, but one problem kept recurring, namely, the probability of selecting a statement from any of the above categories changes for *each* individual (as will be demonstrated shortly).

Finally, it became obvious that if the hypothesis were to be tested properly, the test would have to take into account the individual probabilities of each subject. This automatically ruled out any standard statistical test as group parameters were inappropriate.

The procedure finally developed is described here through the use of an illustration. Looking at the way a subject Q sorted his statements, it was found that 10 of his statements were both relevant and salient. Operationally this means that he placed 10 of the 18 relevant statements into the extreme piles defined as salient. Eight statements were left which were relevant but not salient, and eight which were salient but not relevant.

Next, the subject asked for (bought) eight statements which were distributed so that five of the eight were both relevant and salient; one was relevant only, two were salient only, and none were in the "neither" category. The question then becomes, "What is the joint probability of this distribution?" The question is resolved:

$$\binom{10}{5} \ \binom{8}{1} \ \binom{8}{2} \ \binom{10}{0} \ / \ \binom{36}{8} \ = .00186[1]$$

Once the probability is found for one individual, it can likewise be computed for each of the 80.

Summarizing these 80 probabilities, one finds that the mean probability is .04772, which provides clear support for the hypothesis. Another way of looking at the probability indicates that only 20 of the 80 subjects had a

---

[1] In effect this notation says, "What is the joint probability of selecting 5 statements from 10, 1 statement from 8, 2 statements from 8 and 0 statements from 10 divided by the number of ways you can select 8 statements from 36?"

probability of statement selection greater than .05, with .31 being the highest.[2]

A final way of looking at the data is to note that of the 374 statements bought, 178 (46%) were both relevant and salient; 114 (32%) were relevant only; 45 (12%) were salient only, and 37 (10%) were neither relevant nor salient.

All in all, it is safe to conclude that the information bought was, in fact, a function of the information's salience and relevance. In fact, when the total number of statements are looked at, as in the above paragraph, there is even the suggestion that salience and relevance may work together additively to increase the likelihood that a statement will be chosen.

Descriptive Data:

Machiavellianism. In the next chapter the performances of subjects high and low on Machiavellianism will be compared on several criteria. It is, therefore, important to see what the disposition of Machiavellianism was in this study.

The two instruments measuring Machiavellianism were combined to yield one score. The Mach V instrument has a range of 0 to 20, and the Mach IV a range of 20 to 140. The Mach V was converted to the same range as the Mach IV by multiplying each Mach V score by six and adding twenty. Combining the scores on the instruments yielded a possible range of 40 to 280. The actual range of the subjects in this study was 81 to 244 with a median of 160.5. The distribution of means and standard deviations of the four high Mach groups and the four low Mach groups is described in Table B (p. 76).

The manipulation check. Much of the discussion in the next chapter relies on the effectiveness of the experimental induction in creating a stimulus person who is seen by the subjects as being either highly competitive or highly cooperative. The assumption is that those Q-sort items which Christie selected to describe the High Mach (see Appendix VI) are also indicative of a highly competitive person.

Two sets of data support this assumption; first, those from the semantic differential item, "cooperative-competitive," which was completed by the subjects in the context of 27 other items. Thirty-five of the 40 individuals receiving the competitive set described the hypothetical Other as competitive; and 34 of the 40 individuals receiving the cooperative set described the hypothetical Other as cooperative. None of the 11 other individuals was more

---

[2] Of those 20 subjects, 11 asked for two or fewer statements. Asking for fewer than two statements automatically increases an individual's probability because it decreases the denominator asymmetrically. For instance, notice the decrease in the following denominators:

$$\binom{36}{5} = 378,992 \quad \binom{36}{4} = 58,905 \quad \binom{36}{3} = 7,140 \quad \binom{36}{2} = 630 \quad \binom{36}{1} = 36$$

than one scale point on the side of zero opposite from that expected. The Chi-squares[3] for both High and Low Machs on this item were significant at the .05 level.

Additional evidence that the created sets were effective is presented in Tables C and D (pp. 76, 77). The data for these tables come from the instrument which asked the subjects to estimate the percentage of time that the Other would produce red, blue, or black products (see Appendix VIII). The first impression is recorded after the subject buys any portion of the 36 statements. The set is actually created in the second impression when the subject receives the basic 10 statements, although Tables C and D show that the sets are fairly well created even by the very limited number of statements that the subjects received in the first impression. This is partly due, as might be expected, to the rather high overlap between the statements bought in forming the first impression and the ten statements given in the second impression. The actual count is: of 374 statements requested by the 80 subjects, the 10 basic ones were requested 188 times in the first impression condition.

Both sources of data indicate that the intended manipulation was highly effective. In addition to the continuum, competitive-cooperative, subjects perceived the hypothetical Others to be clearly differentiated along such dimensions as: good-bad, passive-active, dishonest-honest, sensitive-insensitive and other continua noted in Tables E and F (pp. 77, 78).[4]

Summary

This chapter has shown that the major hypothesis is well supported and that the manipulation of the stimulus person was effective.

---

[3] The Chi-squares were computed using the Pearson technique. A tabulation of whether an individual marked the right side or left side of the scale was made. These frequencies were then compared with what might be expected by chance.

[4] The Pearson Chi-squares in Tables E and F were computed by tabulating the number of individuals who checked the scale nearest the right hand word or the left hand word. The resulting distribution was then compared to the distribution expected by chance.

IV

Further Exploratory Results

Focus of This Chapter

The position has been taken in this study that behavior is a function of person and situational properties. In taking this position and in having demonstrated support for the major hypothesis, the object of this chapter is to explore the data in order to understand what the behavioral results of having formed an impression are. The results will be examined by: (1) separating the effects due to the perceiver, the stimulus person, and the situation and (2) studying the interactions among the perceiver, the stimulus person, and the situation.

It was also intended that the design for this portion of the study be heuristic. As this chapter unfolds, special attention will be given to the implications that the data have for continued research and thought concerning person perception.

Format

The organization of this chapter involves a series of contrasts and comparisons. Beginning with a comparison of the way in which High and Low Machs bargain, the discussion then proceeds to examine differences between the way in which High and Low Machs perceive similar stimulus persons.

Next, the interactions among Machiavellianism, the perception of Others and interpersonal bargaining will be discussed in depth.

The Person Property

The High Mach as a bargainer. What kind of a bargainer is the High Mach? Some investigators have found evidence that the High Mach will play to maximize the difference between his payoff and the Other's even when he could increase his total payoff by playing more cooperatively.[1] Is this true of the High Machs in this study? Figure 3 indicates that the answer is neither yes nor no.[2]

Taking red color production as the indicator of competitiveness, High Machs produce more than Low Machs; the overall means are respectively 1.85 and 1.53. However, separate analyses of variance between High and Low Machs for each color produced showed no significant effects due to own Mach orientation. Thus, one is inclined to conclude that there are no differences in this aspect of bargaining behavior between these High and Low Machs.

However, while the overall differences in competitive behavior between High and Low Machs do not seem significant, there is a suggestion that the Highs and Lows may differ in another way; High Machs have a tendency to return the program's own behavior more frequently. This is partly illustrated by the fact that following the attack (Round 10) the forty High Machs attacked the program 57 times as contrasted with the Low's 40 times.

Four other indicators are: (1) The High Machs increase their red production faster following the Other's attack (Round 10). (2) The High Machs decrease their green production faster than the Low Machs following the insepction in Round 14. (They have learned that the program played no red products in Rounds 7 through 14). (3) The High Machs' greater red production in Rounds 21 through 27 reflects the fact that in order to make a profitable attack, one needs more reds because the program is playing a heavy green and blue strategy. (4) The spurt of blue production by the High Machs in Rounds 27 through 35 allows them to maximize the use of the program's blue production.

Again, while none of these differences is significant, they do suggest the interesting hypothesis that the High Mach may be more responsive to the Other than is the Low Mach in this interpersonal bargaining game. This hypothesis would certainly be in keeping with the idea that the High Mach is one who "gets the most out of situation." However, it should be pointed out that the High Machs did not "get the most out of *this* situation."

The mean amount of money earned by Low Machs in the first 35 rounds was $1.18 which was significantly larger than the High Machs' mean earnings of $1.02. While this seems contradictory, Figure 1 suggests why it is not. In Rounds 25 through 28 the High Machs, after having increased their attack behavior, also increase their defensive behavior. This suggests that they are expecting retaliation. This is a very logical expectation which is supported by the subjects'

---

[1] Personal conversation with Richard Christie.

[2] Recall that the subjects are playing against a program which attacks them on the tenth round (indicated by the vertical dotted line) and then the program produces no more red products, while increasing its productions of green and blue products. Also recall that the colors have the following meaning: red = competitive, green = defensive, blue = cooperative, and black = individualistic. Finally, it should be remembered that the subject is allowed to inspect the Other's production on rounds 7, 14, 21, 28 and 35. (The complete program is contained in Appendix V. Figures 1-6 are on pp. 55-60.)

Table 3. Frequency of Statements Asked for by High and Low Machs[a]

Statement	Chosen by High Machs	Chosen by Low Machs	Total
1. I favor conservative values in a variety of areas.	17	17	34
2. I have a wide range of interests.	2	1	3
3. I am not comfortable when others tell me what to do.	3	3	6
4. I enjoy riding in the country.	1	0	1
5. I value power for myself and in others.	17	16	33
6. I tend to relate to everyone in the same way.	1	3	4
7. I enjoy taking mechanical things apart to see how they work.	1	2	3
8. I am a genuinely happy person.	2	0	2
9. I am uncomfortable with uncertainty and complexity.	12	11	23
10. I behave in a giving way towards others.	9	9	18
11. I pride myself on being able to get the most out of any situation.	11	11	22
12. I tend to withdraw where possible in the face of frustration and adversity.	5	5	10
13. I am basically distrustful of people in general; I question their motivations.	12	12	24
14. I have a rapid personal tempo. I behave and act quickly.	6	4	10
15. I pride myself on being very objective and rational.	7	6	13
16. I find it pleasurable to listen to piano music.	0	0	0
17. I initiate humor.	1	1	2
18. I usually read through most of the daily newspaper.	0	0	0
19. I am unpredictable and changeable in behavior.	15	16	31
20. I am concerned with my own adequacy as a person.	4	1	5
21. I enjoy mending broken objects.	0	1	1
22. I am warm and form especially close relationships.	5	4	9
23. I am resistent to anything that can be construed as a demand.	3	3	6
24. I attend many dramatic performances.	2	0	2
25. I am especially alert to differences between myself and other people.	3	2	5
26. I enjoy photography.	1	0	1
27. I enjoy reading well written mystery books.	1	0	1
28. I seek reassurance from others.	3	1	4
29. I behave in a morally consistent manner.	4	11	15
30. I tend to arouse liking and acceptance in people.	4	4	8
31. I may mislead others in order to succeed.	14	18	32
32. I am physically attractive and good looking.	o	3	3
33. I enjoy working with wooden shapes and designs.	2	2	4
34. I am verbally fluent. I can express my ideas well.	0	3	3
35. I am reluctant to commit myself to a definite course of action.	12	13	25
36. I am critical, skeptical, not easily impressed.	5	6	11
TOTAL	184	190	374

[a]These statements were believed to be self-characterizations made by the Other.

own earlier behavior when the program attacked in the Tenth Round. The High Mach Subjects' lower payoff is, therefore, more a consequence of the non-contingent nature of the program (that is, the program plays the same way *regardless* of the subjects' behavior) than it is a reflection of the High Mach Subjects' bargaining skill.

The High Mach as a perceiver. What has been learned about the way in which High Machs perceive Others? First of all, it was noted in the last chapter that there were no differences between High and Low Machs in terms of the hypothesis (seeking information as a function of its salience and relevance). Another similarity between High and Low Machs is that they asked for the same amount of information about the Other. The High Machs asked for 184 statements, the Lows 190; this difference was not significant. The mean number of statements, 4.67 per person, is small; this supports the research cited in Chapter One, which found that persons have a predilection for using relatively few dimensions in forming an impression of an Other.

Table 3 lists the frequencies of the statements which were asked for by High and Low Machs. By and large, it appears that the similarities between Highs and Lows exceed the differences.

While it would not be appropriate to try to treat the fact that seven more Low Machs asked for the statement, "I behave in a morally consistent manner," as a real difference, it does raise the interesting idea that maybe Low Machs approach Others perceptually with more of an evaluative orientation than do High Machs.

In Table 4 none of the words, good-bad, disreputable-reputable, and sensitive-insensitive, which typically load highly on Osgood's evaluative factor have significant Chi-squares for the High Machs. For the Low Machs, however, the evaluative terms are significant. This suggests that the Low Mach orients himself toward Others by evaluating the Other. The High Mach, on the other hand, seems oriented toward the potency and activity dimensions as seen in the Chi-squares, fast-slow, weak-strong, aggressive-defensive.[3]

This suggestion is congruent with the Machiavellian tendency to view Others as objects to be manipulated. For, if one wishes to manipulate an Other, it is probably more important to know how potent the Other is than it is to know that the Other is basically a good or bad person.

Further, if the assumption is made that one indication of sensitivity to an Other's potency might be one's estimate of how many red products the Other is going to produce, then the results in Table 5 are instructive.

Notice the assumption is not being made that the High Mach is *overestimating*

---

[3] A difficulty with making this tentative interpretation is that there is not a uniform independent variable contributing to the Chi-squares. The subjects were free to choose from the thirty-six statements so they had variable bits of information with which to form an impression. However, referring back to Table 3, it is evident that as groups the High and Low Machs had access to pretty much the same information.

Table 4. High and Low Mach Differences In First
Impressions of Others on Semantic Differential

| | High Mach (N=40)[a] | | | | | Low Mach (N=40)[a] | | | | |
| | Expects High Other | | Expects Low Other | | | Expects High Other | | Expects Low Other | | |
Items	Left	Right	Left	Right	X^2	Left	Right	Left	Right	X^2
Good – Bad	9	4	15	1	1.5	9	7	17	0	7.0*
Sensitive – Insensitive	6	10	13	5	2.8	6	11	19	11	14.8*
Light – Heavy	2	3	7	4	0.1	1	11	5	1	4.7*
Masculine – Feminine	13	2	8	8	3.2	16	1	6	8	7.5
Fast – Slow	14	2	6	7	4.0*	16	3	4	8	0.5
Weak – Strong	2	12	10	7	4.7*	1	14	6	10	2.6
Disreputable – Reputable	1	9	1	16	0.1	5	8	0	15	4.6*
Aggressive – Defensive	15	2	7	11	7.1*	14	6	6	11	3.1
Conservative – Liberal	13	3	7	9	3.3	14	4	7	11	4.0*

[a]Frequencies will not add to 40 because those scoring in center scale point are not included.
*Significant at or beyond the .05 level.

the Other's production. There is no way of knowing whether the High or Low is more "accurate;" it is simply being suggested that greater sensitivity to an Other's potency might lead to the expectation that an Other perceived as competitive would produce a high percentage of red products.

Summary of findings on the person property. So far the data have shown that the similarities in the way High and Low Machs bargain and perceive Others far outweigh the differences. Three tentative hypotheses for further study have been offered: (1) High Machs may be more responsive to the Other person in an interpersonal bargaining situation than Low Machs. (2) Low Machs may be more evaluative in forming an impression of an Other than High Machs, and (3) High Machs may be more oriented to the activity and potency dimensions of Others.

The Effects of the Stimulus Person

Having looked at Machiavellianism in relation to perception and bargaining, this section reverses the relation by looking at modifications in High and Low Mach Subjects' behavior, given a particular impression of an Other.

The most informative data for this section are found in the bargaining which takes place in Rounds 36–42. During these seven Rounds, the High and Low Machs have formed their impressions of the Other and are proceeding to bargain.

55

Frequency of Colors Produced

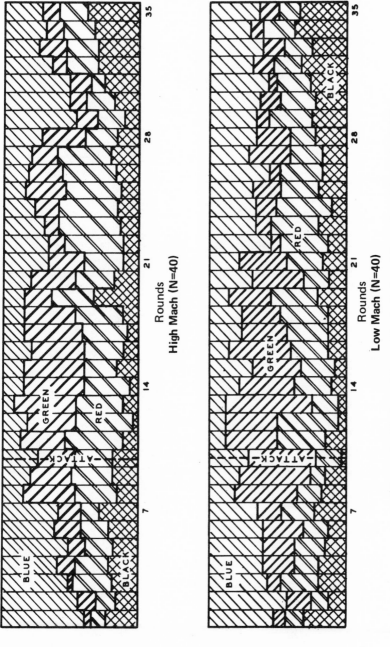

Figure 1. High and Low Mach Color Allocation (Rounds 1-35)

56

Figure 2. High and Low Mach Color Allocation

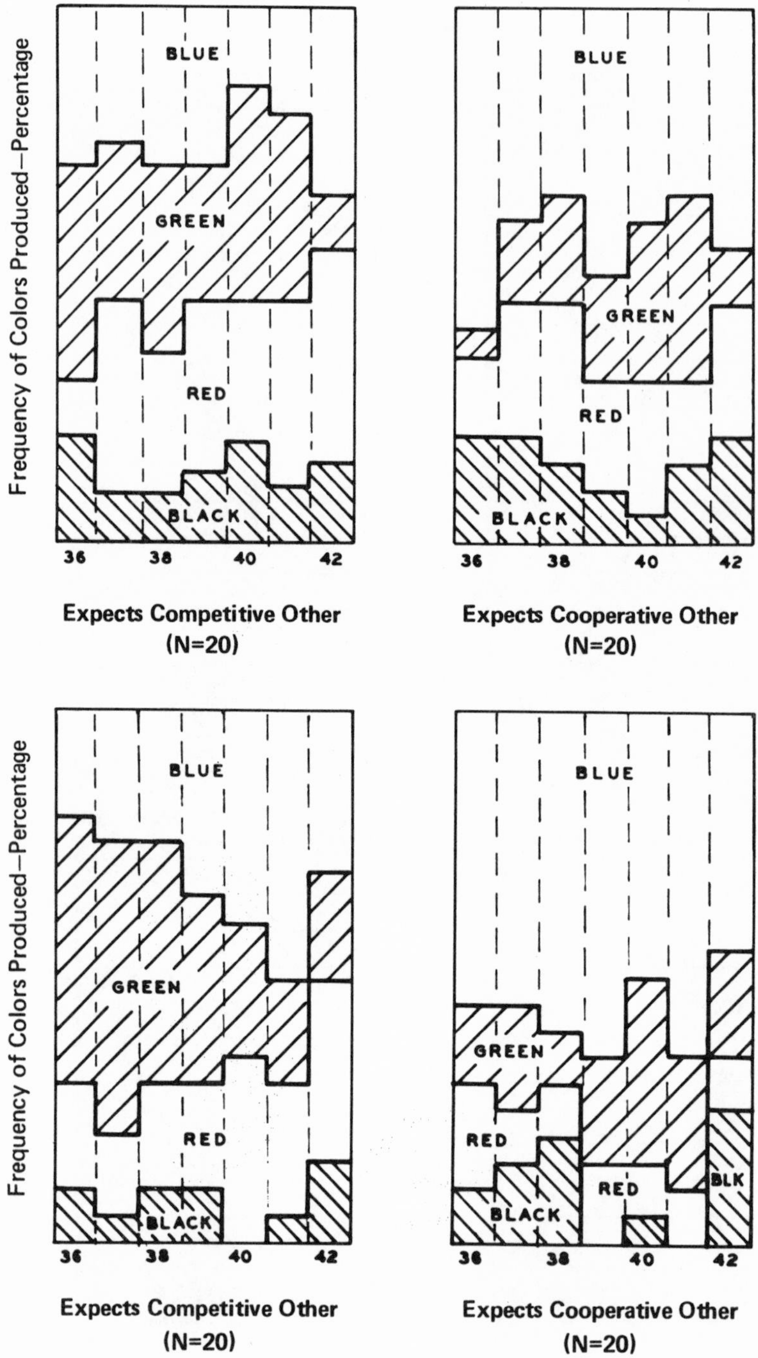

Frequency of Colors Produced

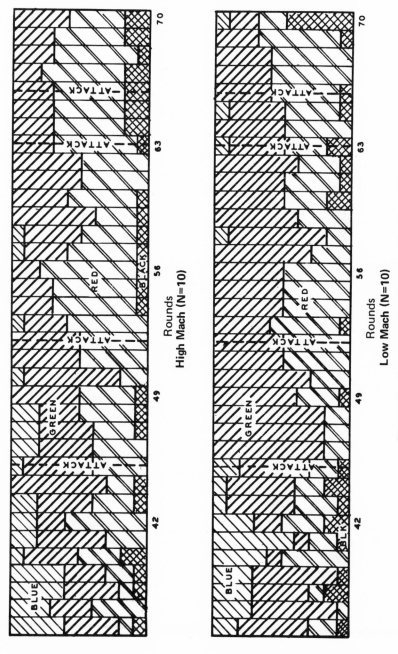

Figure 3. Expects High Other: Confirmed

Frequency of Colors Produced

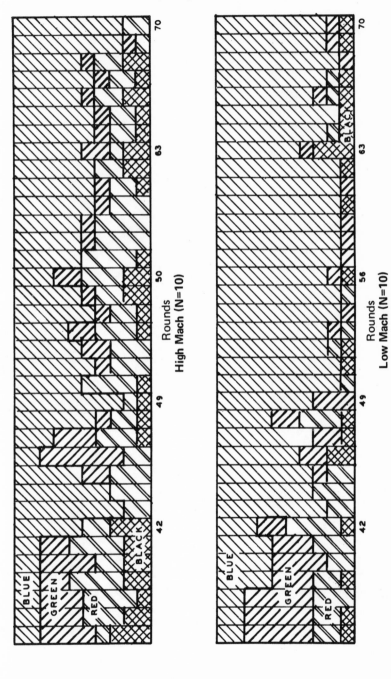

Figure 4. Expects High Other: Disconfirmed

59

Frequency of Colors Produced

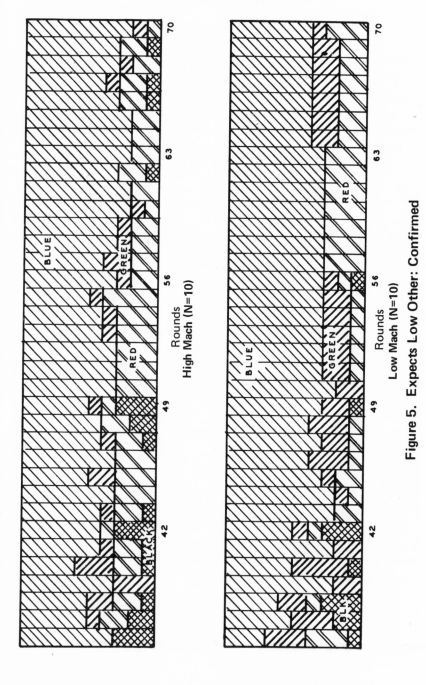

Figure 5. Expects Low Other: Confirmed

Frequency of Colors Produced

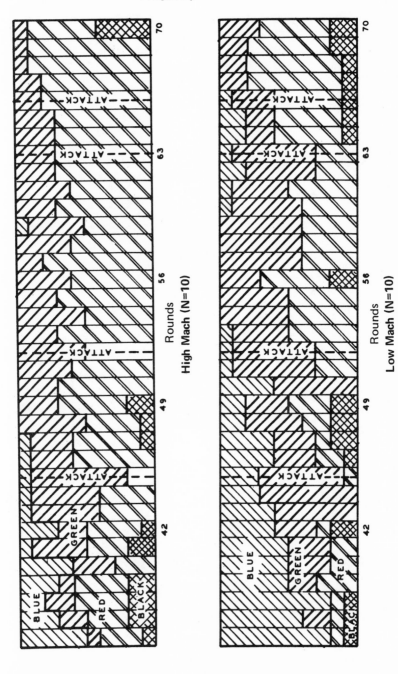

Figure 6. Expects Low Other: Disconfirmed

Up to Round 42 they do not know what the Other is producing. The bargaining behavior is best described in Figure 4.

An analysis of variance (see Tables 6 through 8) suggests what might be inferred from the behavior in this bargaining sequence. Tables 6 and 7 show that the expectation of a High (Competitive) or Low (Cooperative) Other significantly affects the allocation of green and blue products.

Table 8 shows that neither one's own orientation nor his expectation of the Other significantly affects red production. The lack of significant effects in red production before the first inspection is not surprising. A common sense notion of bargaining would suggest that, even when expecting a tough competitor, it is a better strategy to wait until he shows his hand than it is to initiate aggression. Two reasons support the "wait and see" notion: (1) It is possible to fully protect oneself with the green products. (2) To initiate aggression may communicate to the Other that the subject is more competitive than the subject wishes to appear.

The bargaining behavior discussed above illustrates perfectly why it has been stressed in the introduction to this study that a person perception experiment ought to provide an opportunity to see the behavioral consequences of an impression of an Other. If a person will modify his behavior in connection with an impression he has formed of an Other, in a specific situation such as bargaining, the investigator can be much more confident that the study of impression formation will have meaningful behavioral consequences in other settings.

Summary. Looking at the discussion concerning Machiavellianism and perception, and the data in this section which have related Machiavellianism, impression formation and interpersonal bargaining, a generalization is in order. While no clearcut differences were evident between High and Low Machs as perceivers, it has become evident that the consequences of the impressions formed by High and Low Machs do lead to some important behavioral differences in an interpersonal bargaining situation.

The whole area of one bargainer's impressions of Other bargainers needs further exploration. How does the perceived rationality, confidence, or intelligence of the Other affect one's bargaining? Marlow, Gergen and Doob[4] have begun to examine this area. In a study published in 1966 they found that subjects cooperated more with a humble person they expected to meet than with one they did not expect to meet, and, on the other hand, when the partner was perceived as an egotist, there was greater cooperation if they did *not* expect to interact with him.

The Effects of an Impression Confirmed or Disconfirmed

This section is designed to explore what happens to High and Low Mach

---

[4] D. Marlowe, K. Gergen & A. Doob, Opponent's personality, expectation of social interaction, and interpersonal bargaining. *J. pers. soc. Psychol.*, 1966, 2, 206–213.

62

Table 5. High and Low Mach Subjects' Estimates of Red Color[a]
Production by an Expected Competitive Other

| High Mach | | Low Mach | | |
Mean	SD	Mean	SD	t
55.35%	17.55	41.75%	24.59	5.19[b]

[a]For estimations of all colors, see Tables C and D, pp. 76 and 77.
[b]Significant at or beyond the .05 level.

Subjects' bargaining behavior and their impressions of Others when their expectations are either confirmed or disconfirmed.

At the end of Round 42, the first inspection in the last 35 Rounds occurs. The subjects then learn that the Other has either played all blue or all red. The program continues to play all blue or all red with four attacks for the rest of the time. Those expecting a competitive Other, who learn that the Other has played all red, have their expectation confirmed; if the Other has played all blue, their expectation is disconfirmed. The reverse is true for those expecting a cooperative Other. Again, the best way to describe what happens to the bargaining behavior following confirmation or disconfirmation is to plot the actual production behavior. This has been done in Figures 3 through 6. (In Figures 3 and 6, the broken vertical lines indicate when the program attacks the subject.)

Figures 3 and 5 show that both High and Low Machs respond to confirmation of their expectations in about the same way. However, the trend suggested earlier seems to be continuing; Low Machs tend to respond to aggression with

Table 6. Analysis of Variance for Green Color Production on Trial Block 6
for High and Low Machs Expecting High and Low Others

	Sum of Squares	NDF	Mean Square	F	P
Rows[a]	21.0125	1.	21.0125	7.19833	.01
Columns[b]	2.8125	1.	2.8125	.96348	
Inter.	.3125	1.	.3125	.10705	
Error	221.8500	76.	2.9190		
Total	245.9875	79.			

| | Cell Means Own | | | Cell Variances Own | |
	High	Low		High	Low
Expects High	2.15	2.65	Expects High	3.29	4.66
Expects Low	1.25	1.50	Expects Low	1.35	2.36

[a]Expectation of Other effect
[b]Own Mach effect

Table 7. Analysis of Variance for Blue Color Production on Trial Block 6
for High and Low Machs Expecting High and Low Others

	Sum of Squares	NDF	Mean Square	F	P
Rows[a]	46.5125	1.	46.5125	8.51692	.01
Columns[b]	10.5125	1.	10.5125	1.92494	
Inter.	2.1125	1.	2.1125	1.38682	
Error	415.0500	76.	5.4611		
Total	474.1875	79.			

	Cell Means Own			Cell Variances Own	
	High	Low		High	Low
Expects High	1.85	2.25	Expects High	4.99	6.30
Expects Low	3.05	4.10	Expects Low	5.20	5.35

[a]Expectation of Other effect
[b]Own Mach effect

green (defensive) products more than do High Machs. The High Machs, on the other hand, are producing more red (aggressive) products than the Low Machs.

What Figures 3 through 6 do not show is that Low Machs are basically defensive bargainers and High Machs are basically aggressive bargainers. To demonstrate this, three-way analyses of variance (conditions X Mach X trial blocks) were run on the last 28 rounds of bargaining. The High Mach Subjects' basic aggressiveness shows up as a significant main effect in Table 10. The Low

Table 8. Analysis of Variance for Red Color Production on Trial Block 6
for High and Low Machs Expecting High and Low Others

	Sums of Squares	NDF	Mean Square	F	P
Rows[a]	6.6125	1.	6.6125	2.3611	NS
Columns[b]	9.1125	1.	9.1125	3.2537	.05
Inter.	.6125	1.	.6125	.2187	NS
Error	212.8500	76.	2.8006		
Total	229.1875	79.			

	Cell Means Own			Cell Variances Own	
	High	Low		High	Low
Expects High	1.85	1.35	Expects High	2.97	3.39
Expects Low	1.45	.60	Expects Low	2.78	2.04

[a]Expectation of Other effect
[b]Own Mach effect

Table 9. Three-Way Analysis of Variance for Green (Defensive)
Color Production on Trial Blocks 6-10 for High and Low Mach Subjects
in Four Experimental Conditions.

Source	Sums of Squares	DF	Mean Square	F	P
Between Subjects	901.872	79			
(1) Conditions	421.734	3	140.58	23.00	.01
(2) Mach	20.503	1	20.50	3.35	.01
(1) X (2)	19.609	3	6.54	1.07	NS
Error Between Ss	440.026	72	6.11		
Within Cells	886.249	240			
(3) Trial Blocks	36.559	3	12.19	3.30	.05
(1) X (3)	35.078	9	3.90	1.06	NS
(2) X (3)	.284	3	.10	.03	NS
(1) X (2) X (3)	17.053	9	1.91	.51	NS
Error within cells	797.275	216	3.69		

Mach Subjects' defensive behavior almost reaches significance (probability one chance in ten) in Table 9.

This means that the Low Machs' defensive behavior and the High Machs' aggressive behavior in response to aggression is simply an increase in the intensities of their preferred bargaining strategies.

Figures 4 and 6 suggest some differences in the way High and Low Machs respond to disconfirmation of their expectations. For instance, when both groups are expecting a cooperative (low) Other (Figure 6), it takes much longer

Table 10. Three-Way Analysis of Variance for Red (Aggressive)
Color Production on Trial Blocks 6-10 for High and Low Mach Subjects
in Four Experimental Conditions.

Source	Sums of Squares	DF	Mean Square	F	P
Between Subjects	1,415.988	79			
(1) Conditions	328.337	3	109.446	8.00	.01
(2) Mach	82.012	1	82.012	6.00	.05
Conditions X Mach	20.737	3	6.912	0.51	NS
Error Between Ss	984.902	72	13.679		
Within cells	946.999	240			
(3) Trial Blocks	44.862	3	14.954	4.06	.01
(1) X (3)	80.687	9	8.965	2.43	.05
(2) X (3)	4.562	3	1.521	.41	NS
(1) X (2) X (3)	20.987	9	2.332	.63	NS
Error within cells	795.901	216	3.685		

to extinguish the Low Machs' cooperative (blue) behavior than it does for the High Machs.

Figure 4 shows that the High Machs never become as cooperative as the Low Machs when they have anticipated a competitive Other and learned that the Other is actually producing cooperative products. Does this suggest that the High Mach is more distrustful?

The above discussion does not exhaust the interesting phenomena displayed in Figures 3 through 6. It is tempting to explore differences in subjects' responses to aggression (i.e., with counter-aggression or with defensive behavior) in terms of conditions and/or own orientations which increase the need to "save face." For instance, one way of understanding the differential increase in red production between Figure 3, in which a competitive Other is expected and confirmed, and Figure 6, in which a cooperative Other is expected and disconfirmed (note that the Other's *program* behavior is the same for both) is that the disconfirmation leads to embarrassment or "loss of face" which is restored with counter-aggression. The problem with such a general hypothesis is that the increase in red production in the cooperative-disconfirm condition is due entirely to an increase in red production by the High Machs. High Machs in the Expected Low-Disconfirm condition produce 41 more reds in trials 43–70 and attack 8 more times than the High Machs in the Expected High Other-Confirm condition, whereas the Low Machs do not increase their red production and attack 4 *fewer* times than in the expected High Other-Confirm condition. Is it possible that the High Machs who are more oriented *toward* manipulating Others, are also more sensitive to manipulation *by* Others? And does this greater sensitivity lead to a higher need to "save face"? With or without the face-saving rationale, the question is worth exploring.

Summary. While many similarities and differences have been explored in this section, the generalization which seems most significant is: High and Low Machs respond differently in their bargaining behavior to disconfirmation of their expectations. For example, when an anticipated cooperative Other is competitive, High Machs become very aggressive, whereas Low Machs are slow to discontinue their cooperative behavior. Conversely, Low Machs cooperate much more easily with an anticipated competitive Other who is cooperative.

The Impression Formed and its Confirmation or Disconfirmation

Up to this point, the data have been treated as though the production of red or blue colors completely confirms or disconfirms the subjects' expectations about the Other. This is probably legitimate, because the most relevant expectation (whether the Other is competitive or cooperative) was entirely confirmed or disconfirmed. However, the subjects were asked to describe the Other in a series of paired words; these data bear on the total impression formed of the Other.

Table 11. Changes in Impressions Due to a
Disconfirmation of an Expected Competitive Other

| | High Mach (Only) | | | Low Mach (Only)[a] | |
	Second Impression	Third Impression		Second Impression	Third Impression
Passive – Active[a]	5.8[b]	4.7	Light – Heavy	5.2[b]	4.2
Generous – Selfish	5.8	3.9	Awful – Nice	3.4	5.3
Competent – Incompetent	3.1	4.6	Masculine – Feminine	2.3	3.8
Weak – Strong	5.6	4.1			
Complex – Simple	3.5	4.5			
Warm – Cold	5.3	3.7			

[a]The differences in words listed are all significant at the .05 level.
[b]The higher the mean the closer it is to the right hand word.
NOTE: All pairs of words which changed significantly for High Machs *only* or for Low Machs *only* are included. If both High and Low Machs changed significantly, the pair is not included.

The changes in a disconfirmation between impression two (formed just prior to the last 35 rounds of bargaining) and impression three (formed just after the last 35 rounds) are most easily seen by looking at the profiles in Tables G, H, I and J (pp. 79-82).

The differences between the impressions of the groups which did not receive a disconfirmation are not presented because they are so minor. For instance, for the High Machs expecting a cooperative Other, the only change of significance was on the pair of words – awful/nice – and this change was from nice to nicer.

Table 12. Changes in Impressions Due to a
Disconfirmation of an Expected Cooperative Other

| | High Mach (Only) | | | Low Mach (Only) | |
	Second Impression	Third Impression		Second Impression	Third Impression
Good – Bad[a]	2.4	3.9[b]	Sensitive – Insensitive[a]	2.1	3.3[b]
Dishonest – Honest	6.2	4.0	Light – Heavy	3.3	4.4
Awful – Nice	5.8	3.9	Competent – Incompetent	3.2	2.4
	2.5	3.6	Masculine – Feminine	4.6	3.2
			Fast – Slow	3.9	3.1
			Weak – Strong	4.1	5.1

[a]The differneces in words listed are all significant at the .05 level.
[b]The higher the mean the closer it is to the right-hand word.
NOTE: All pairs of words which changed significantly for High Machs *only* or for Low Machs *only* are included. If both High and Low Machs changed significantly, the pair is not included.

(The means were: second impression 5.8 and third impression 6.4) For the Low Machs in the same condition, the cooperative Other was seen as significantly more cooperative between times 2 and 3 and as free rather than constrained. In the other condition, in which High and Low Machs received a confirmation of a competitive Other, there were no significant changes in impression for Low Machs, and the High Machs had only one change: they saw the Other as being more incompetent.

In contrast to the confirmation conditions, the disconfirmation conditions are quite striking. Tables 11 and 12 present the pairs of words for which there were significant mean changes in impressions for either the High or Low Mach groups. They also show the differences between disconfirmations of expected cooperative Others and expected competitive Others.

The differences are intriguing. Why are the High Machs responding to a disconfirmation of a cooperative Other with such evaluative terms which means they now see the Other as bad, dishonest and awful? The High Machs in the early impressions, one and two, were not prone to categorizing Others along the evaluative terms. Also, why are the Low Machs *not* changing significantly on these terms when they are prone to evaluative terms? These questions invite speculation. Assuming, for the moment, that the hypothetical competitive Other in this experiment is seen as similar to oneself by the High Machs, while the hypothetical cooperative Other is seen as similar by the Low Machs, the research literature cited in the first chapter would suggest that those seen as similar are usually liked by the perceiver. Given this assumption, one might hypothesize that when an Other, who is perceived as dissimilar, acts in such a way as to disconfirm one's impression of the Other, disliking for the Other will increase. But, this hypothesis would not explain the results in Table 11. However, if one looks at the results of the disconfirmation of a competitive Other one sees that the proposed hypothesis needs to be revised to read:

> When an Other who is perceived as dissimilar acts in such a way as to disconfirm the perceiver's impression of Other, and the disconfirmation *costs* the perceiver, dislike will increase.

This hypothesis is not surprising except that the implication is that dislike will *not* increase for a perceived *similar* Other who disconfirms the perceiver's impression at a *cost* to the perceiver. (Cost is being used here in the reified sense of any loss of status, face, or prestige.) One needs only to think of the costs of loving another person and the implication makes sense.

Chapter Summary

The purpose of this chapter has been to demonstrate, in a person perception experiment, the usefulness of data which allow the investigator to look at effects caused by the perceiver, the perceived, and the situation, separately and in combination.

Similarities and differences were noted between High and Low Machs as perceivers and as bargainers. For instance, the information selected about the Other was very similar for both High and Low Machs. Also, High and Low Machs in bargaining with an Other who was unknown proved to be quite similar, with the exception that High Machs tended to respond in kind to changes in the Other's bargaining.

In initial impressions formed, High Machs tended to categorize Others along potency and activity dimensions, whereas Low Machs were more evaluative.

When asked to estimate how competitive a competitive Other would be, High Machs saw the Other as one who should play aggressively, more so than did Low Machs making estimations for the same competitive Other.

Having formed an impression that the Other was either competitive or cooperative markedly altered the bargaining behavior of both High and Low Machs.

Low Machs proved, generally, to take a defensive stance toward Others, while High Machs proved to be more aggressive. Confirmation and disconfirmation of the way in which the Other was expected to bargain was reacted to differently by High and Low Machs. For example, High Machs anticipating a competitive Other who turns out to be cooperative are not as cooperative as the Low Machs in the same condition.

Finally, the types of changes in impression which resulted from a behavioral disconfirmation of expectations are somewhat different for High and Low Machs.

Concluding Comments

This study started with a comprehensive review of the person preception literature, narrowed its focus to a single impression formation hypothesis and then explored the effects of the impression coupled with Machiavellianism upon interpersonal bargaining behavior.

As concluding remarks, a final question will be posed and the hypotheses which need testing will be suggested. This type of conclusion seems fitting in that it respects the intention of the design to be heuristic.

The major question. In interpersonal bargaining, what are the important person perception variables involved in the establishment of cooperation among persons who have a high Machiavellian orientation? In order to respond to this question, the following hypotheses need to be tested:

(1) In an interpersonal bargaining situation, in which the Other is unknown, persons of a high Machiavellian orientation will have a greater tendency to escalate conflict than to resolve it.

(2) In an interpersonal bargaining situation, in which the characteristics of each bargainer are known, cooperation will be more easily attained when two bargainers mutually perceive each other as competitive, than when one is perceived as competitive and the other is perceived as cooperative.

(3) In an interpersonal bargaining situation, persons with a high Machiavellian orientation will be more effective with an Other whose strategy is highly variable than will a person of low Machiavellian orientation.

(4) To increase cooperation in an interpersonal bargaining situation with persons of high Machiavellian orientation, it is important to structure the situation so that the High Mach has an opportunity to inspect the Other's actual cooperative behavior before the Other inspects the High Mach's behavior.

(5) In an interpersonal bargaining situation, persons who have a high Machiavellian orientation will react more aggressively to a manipulatory act by an Other than will persons of low Machiavellian orientation.

(6) In an interpersonal bargaining situation, persons who perceive each other as similar on salient characteristics will attain cooperation more easily than persons who see each other as dissimilar on salient characteristics.

It is hoped that by concluding with these hypotheses, the reader will share with the investigator a sense of a task not yet complete.

V

Summary

Person perception studies have, in general, not offered comprehensive coverage of the problem. They tend to focus on one of its aspects, be it the perceived, the perceiver, or the situation, and neglect to weigh the relative contributions of each of these factors to the totality of the problem.

Few person perception studies reviewed made any attempt to see if the categories used by the experimenter were salient for the subject. No study reviewed determined whether salience varies with individuals in the same situation, or whether it varies as a function of the situation, or both, under differing conditions.

Two other areas which have been inadequately covered in the literature to date are situations in which the perceiver interacts with the perceived and situations in which the degree of accuracy of one's perception has behavioral consequences for the perceiver.

A laboratory design was created to test the hypothesis:

In forming an impression of an Other, the perceiver will seek information that is a function of its *salience* to the perceiver and its *relevance* to the situation in which the impression is formed.

Also, by creating a design which permitted sequential assessment of the relationships of the impressions formed to the: (1) relevant properties of the perceiver, (2) variations in the stimulus person, and (3) differences in situational elements, it was possible to plan for and discuss results which were not related to specific hypotheses.

Procedures

Eighty subjects were given two scales which measure Machiavellianism. The subjects were split at the median into High and Low Mach groups. Each group was again split into two groups, one of which received an impression of a competitive Other; the other group received an impression of a cooperative Other. The subjects then participated in an interpersonal bargaining game against a program which either confirmed or disconfirmed their expectation that the Other was competitive or cooperative.

Results

The major hypothesis was supported at the .05 level of confidence. Statistical checks showed all the manipulations to be effective.

In addition, similarities and differences were noted between High and Low Machs as perceivers and as bargainers. For example, the information selected about an Other was very similar for both High and Low Machs. Also, High and Low Machs in bargaining with an Other who was unknown proved to be quite similar in their behavior, with the exception that Low Machs tended to respond to aggression with defensive behavior whereas Highs responded with counter-aggression. There was also a tendency for High Machs to respond more quickly, and to respond more in kind, to changes in the Other's bargaining.

In impressions formed, High Machs tended to categorize Others along Osgood's potency and activity dimensions whereas Low Machs were more evaluative.

In estimating how a competitive Other would bargain, High Machs anticipated the Other would be more aggressive than did the Low Machs.

Forming an impression that the Other was cooperative led Low and High Machs to increase their own cooperativeness, but much more so for Lows than Highs. Anticipating a competitive Other led Low Machs to be defensive and High Machs to be aggressive.

When an anticipated cooperative Other bargained competitively, High Machs evaluated the Other much more negatively than did the Low Machs.

The study succeeded in taking a comprehensive view of a single person perception hypothesis and concluded that, within the limits of this experiment, persons form impressions in very similar ways, but the expectations created by those impressions interact with one's own Machiavellian orientation resulting in quite different behavioral responses within an interpersonal bargaining situation.

References

Ager, J. W. & Dawes, F. M. The effect of judges' attitudes on judgment. *J. Pers. soc. Psychol.*, 1965, 1, 533–539.

Altrocchi, J. Interpersonal perceptions of repressors and sensitizers and component analysis of assumed dissimilarity scores. *J. abnorm. soc. Psychol.*, 1961, 62, 528–535.

Asch, S. E. Forming impressions of personality. *J. abnorm. soc. Psychol.*, 1946, 41, 258–290.

Asch, S. E. *Social psychology*. New York: Prentice-Hall, 1952.

Backman, C. W. & Secord, P. F. The effect of perceived liking on interpersonal attraction. *Human Relations*, 1959, 12, 379–386.

Beach, L. & Wertheimer, M. A. Free response approach to the study of person cognition. *J. abnorm. soc. Psychol.*, 1961, 62, 367–374.

Benedetti, D. T. & Hill, J. G. A determiner of the centrality of a trait in impression formation. *J. abnorm. soc. Psychol.*, 1960, 60, 278–280.

Berlew, D. E. & Williams, A. F. Interpersonal sensitivity under motive arousing conditions. *J. abnorm. soc. Psychol.*, 1964, 68, 150–160.

Block, J. *The Q-sort method in personality assessment and psychiatric research*. Springfield, Ill.: Charles C. Thomas, 1961.

Boring, E. G. *History, psychology, and science; selected papers.* New York: John Wiley, 1963.

Brammel, D. A dissonance theory approach to defensive projection. *J. abnorm. soc. Psychol.*, 1962, 64, 121–129.

Brown, R. *Social psychology*. New York: The Free Press, 1965.

Bruner, J. S. & Postman, L. Perception, cognition and behavior. *J. Pers.*, 1949, 18, 14–31.

Bruner, J. S. & Taguiuri, R. The perception of people. In G. Lindzey (Ed.), *Handbook of social psychology*. Vol. 2. *Special fields and applications*. Cambridge, Mass.: Addison-Wesley, 1954. p. 634–654.

Bruner, J. S. Going beyond the information given. In Jessor, et. al. (Eds.), *A Symposium on Cognition*. Cambridge, Mass.: Harvard University Press, 1957.

Bruner, J. S., Shapiro, D. & Tagiuri, R. The meaning of traits in isolation and in combination. In R. Tagiuri & L. Petrullo (Eds.), *Person perception and interpersonal behavior.* Stanford: Stanford University Press, 1958. Pp. 277–289.

Brunswik, E. *The conceptual framework of psychology*. Chicago: University of Chicago Press, 1952.

Byrne, D. Interpersonal attraction and attitude similarity. *J. abnorm. soc. Psychol.*, 1961, 62, 713–715.

72

Byrne, D. & Blaylock, B. Similarity and assumed similarity of attitudes between husbands and wives. *J. abnorm. soc. Psychol.*, 1963, 67, 636–640.

Cantril, H. Perception and interpersonal relations. In E. P. Hollander & R. G. Hunt (Eds.), *Current perspectives in social psychology*. New York: Oxford University Press, 1963. Pp. 290–298.

Carlson, E. R. Motivation and set in acquiring information about persons. *J. Pers.*, 1961, 29, 285–293.

Cassirer, E. *Substance and function*. Chicago: Open Court, 1923.

Christie, R. Impersonal interpersonal orientations and behavior. Research Proposal. NSF, 1962.

Cline, V. B. & Richards, J. M., Jr. Accuracy of interpersonal perception: a general trait? *J. abnorm. soc. Psychol.*, 1960, 60, 1–7.

Cline, V. B. & Richards, J. M., Jr. Cline and Richards' reply to O'Connor's methodological note. *J. abnorm. soc. Psychol.*, 1963, 66, 195.

Cronbach, L. J. Processes affecting scores on "understanding of others" and "assumed similarity." *Psychol. Bull.*, 1955, 52, 177–194.

Cronbach, L. J. Proposals leading to analytic treatment of social perception scores. In R. Tagiuri & L. Petrullo (Eds.), *Person perception and interpersonal behavior*. Stanford: Stanford University Press, 1958. Pp. 353–379.

Crow, W. J. & Hammond, K. R. The generality of accuracy and response sets in interpersonal perception. *J. abnorm. soc. Psychol.*, 1957, 54, 384–396.

Deutsch, M. & Hornstein, H. A. The tendencies to compete and to attack as a function of inspection, incentive, and available alternatives. (Mimeo.), 1965.

Deutsch, M. & Krauss, R. Studies of interpersonal bargaining. *J. confl. Resol.*, 1962, 6, 52–76.

Deutsch, M. & Krauss, R. *Theories in social psychology*. New York: Basic Books, 1965.

Gordon, J. E. The stability of the assumed similarity response set in repressors and sensitizers. *J. Pers.*, 1959, 27, 362–373.

Hastorf, A. H., Dornbusch, S. M., et. al. The perceiver and the perceived: their relative influence on the categories of interpersonal cognition. *J. Pers. soc. Psychol.*, 1965, 1, 434–440.

Hastorf, A. H., Richardson, S. A. & Dornbusch, S. M. The problem of relevance in the study of person perception. In R. Tagiuri & L. Petrullo (Eds.), *Person perception and interpersonal behavior*. Stanford: Stanford University Press, 1958. Pp. 54–63.

Heider, F. *The psychology of interpersonal relations*. New York: John Wiley, 1958.

Holmes, D. S. & Berkowitz, L. Some contrast effects in social perception. *J. abnorm. soc. Psychol.*, 1961, 62, 150–153.

Iverson, M. A. Personality impressions of punitive stimulus persons of differential status. *J. abnorm. soc. Psychol.*, 1964, 68, 617–626.

Jackson, D. N. & Messick, S. Individual differences in social perception. *Brit. J. soc. clin. Psychol.*, 1963, 1–10.

Jones, E. E., Gergen, K. J. & Davis, K. E. Some determinants of reactions to being approved or disapproved as a person. *Psychol. Monogr.*, 1962, 76, (2, Whole no. 521), 17 pp.

Loeb, A., Feshbach, S., Beck, A. T. & Wolf, A. Some effects of reward upon the social perception and motivation of psychiatric patients varying in depression. *J. abnorm. soc. Psychol.*, 1964, 68, 609–617.

Marlowe, D., Gergen, K. & Doob, S. A. Opponent's personality, expectation of social interaction, and interpersonal bargaining. *J. of pers. soc. Psychol.* 1966, 2, 206–213.

Newcomb, T. M. *The acquaintance process*. New York: Holt, Rinehart & Winston, 1961.

Newcomb, T. M. Stabilities underlying changes in interpersonal attraction. *J. abnorm. soc. Psychol.*, 1963, 66, 376–386.

74

Newcomb, T. M., Turner, R. H. & Converse, P. E. *Social psychology*. New York: Holt, Rinehart & Winston, 1965.

O'Connor, W. F. A methodological note on the Cline and Richards' studies on accuracy of interpersonal perception. *J. abnorm. soc. Psychol.*, 1963, 66, 194–195.

Osgood, C. E. *Method and theory in experimental psychology*. New York: Oxford University Press, 1953.

Postman, L. The probability approach and nomothetic theory. *Psychol. Rev.*, 1955, 62, 218–225.

Pyron, B. Accuracy of interpersonal perception as a function of consistency of information. *J. Pers. soc. Psychol.*, 1965, 1, 111–118.

Rodgers, D. A. Relationship between real similarity and assumed similarity with favorability controlled. *J. abnorm. soc. Psychol.*, 1959, 59, 431–433.

Sarbin, T. Role theory. In G. Lindzey (Eds.), *Handbook of social psychology*. Vol. 2. *Special fields and applications*. Cambridge, Mass.: Addison-Wesley, 1954.

Secord, P. F. & Backman, C. W. *Social psychology*. New York: McGraw-Hill, 1964.

Secord, P. F., Backman, C. W. & Eachus, H. T. Effects of imbalance in the self concept on the perception of persons. *J. abnorm. soc. Psychol.*, 1964, 68, 442–446.

Shrauger, S. & Altrocchi, J. The personality of the perceiver as a factor in person perception. *Psychol. Bull.*, 1964, 62, 291.

Taft, R. The ability to judge people. *Psychol. Bull.*, 1955, 52, 1–24.

Tagiuri, R. Introduction. In R. Tagiuri & L. Petrullo (Eds.), *Person perception and interpersonal behavior*. Stanford: Stanford University Press, 1958.

Thompson, D. F. & Meltzer, L. Communication of emotional intent by facial expression. *J. abnorm. soc. Psychol.*, 1964, 68, 129–135.

Zajonc, R. B. The process of cognitive tuning in communication. *J. abnorm. soc. Psychol.*, 1960, 61, 159–167.

Tables A-J

Table A. Distribution of Statements Selected by Subjects
According to the Q-Sort Piles from which they were Selected

Q-Sort Pile	Expected[a] Distribution	Empirical Distribution
Extremely Characteristic	21	32
Quite Characteristic	31	32
Fairly Characteristic	41	41
Somewhat Characteristic	52	37
About Equally Characteristic and Uncharacteristic	84	83
Somewhat Uncharacteristic	52	33
Fairly Uncharacteristic	41	37
Quite Uncharacteristic	31	41
Extremely Uncharacteristic	21	38
Total	374	374

[a]The expected distribution is computed by determining how many chances each statement has of being drawn from each category. Thus, since there are two statements placed in an end category, the probability of drawing one of those statements if 2 out of 36 or .0555. And (.0555) (374) = 20.76.

Table B. Means and Standard Deviations of Mach Scores by Condition

Condition	High Mach (N=40) Mean	SD	Low Mach (N=40) Mean	SD
Expects High Other: Confirmed	183.80	14.73	127.40	20.27
Expects High Other: Disconfirmed	188.20	24.65	138.60	12.32
Expects Low Other: Confirmed	182.40	17.97	138.60	21.81
Expects Low Other: Disconfirmed	191.60	17.72	133.20	25.17

[a]Variances are homogeneous within High and Low Mach groups.

Table C. High Mach Subjects' Anticipations of Others' Color
Production: First and Second Impressions
(N=40)

Expects High (N=20) First Impression	Second Impression	Color Estimated	Expects Low (N=20) First Impression	Second Impression
46.85%	55.35%	Red (Competitive)	21.61%	16.65%
28.50%	22.50%	Blue (Cooperative)	57.79%	59.60%
24.40%	22.15%	Black (Individual)	21.05%	23.75%

Table D. Low Mach Subjects' Anticipations of Others' Color
Production: First and Second Impressions
(N=40)

Expects High (N=20)		Color	Expects Low (N=20)	
First Impression	Second Impression	Estimated	First Impression	Second Impression
40.48%	41.75%	Red (Competitive)	22.50%	18.75%
30.48%	29.75%	Blue (Cooperative)	54.75%	60.50%
29.05%	28.50%	Black (Individual)	22.25%	20.75%

Table E. High Mach Frequency and Chi-Square of Semantic Differential Items

Semantic Items Left Right	Expects High Other Left	Right	Expects Low Other Left	Right	X^2
Good/bad	5	8	16	0[a]	10.7*
Passive/active	2	17	11	6	9.2*
Dishonest/honest	13	2	0	19	23.1*
Sensitive/insensitive	3	15	17	3	15.1*
Light/heavy	2	7	10	3	4.4*
Generous/selfish	1	17	19	0	29.5*
Hostile/peaceful	19	1	0	18	30.5*
Competent/incompetent	14	3	8	5	0.7
Soft/hard	2	14	15	0	20.5*
Wise/foolish	9	6	17	3	1.6
Suspicious/trusting	18	0	3	16	23.4*
Constrained/free	10	9	9	10	0.0
Awful/nice	7	3	0	17	12.6*
Open/closed	4	15	8	6	3.1
Masculine/feminine	14	3	5	11	6.8*
Cooperative/competitive	0	19	18	1	30.5*
Fast/slow	15	2	6	7	4.4*
Small/large	6	4	8	2	0.2
Clean/dirty	11	2	13	0	0.5
Weak/strong	2	16	11	4	10.8*
Yielding/unyielding	1	17	17	2	22.8*
Disreputable/reputable	8	5	0	17	11.3
Brave/cowardly	12	5	8	6	0.2
Aggressive/defensive	19	1	3	12	17.6*
Conservative/liberal	13	4	9	8	1.2
Complex/simple	9	5	5	8	.9
Warm/cold	1	16	15	0	24.6*

*Significant at or beyond the .05 level.
[a]Center scale point not included, so frequencies do not necessarily add to 40.

Table F. Low Mach Frequency and Chi-Square of Semantic Differential Items

Semantic Items Left Right	Expects High Other Left	Right	Expects Low Other Left	Right	X^2
Good/bad	2	12	17	0[a]	20.3*
Passive/active	2	18	12	7	9.8*
Dishonest/honest	15	3	1	16	18.1*
Sensitive/insensitive	4	16	19	1	20.0*
Light/heavy	2	9	7	5	2.3
Generous/selfish	2	17	17	1	22.8*
Hostile/peaceful	15	4	1	19	19.1*
Competent/incompetent	14	2	10	3	0.1
Soft/hard	1	16	14	1	21.1*
Wise/foolish	9	7	12	2	1.8
Suspicious/trusting	18	2	2	18	22.5*
Constrained/free	10	8	11	7	0.0
Awful/nice	8	3	1	15	10.1*
Open/closed	7	12	13	6	2.6
Masculine/feminine	19	0	4	10	16.2*
Cooperative/competitive	1	19	17	2	24.7*
Fast/slow	18	2	8	4	1.4
Small/large	4	6	2	3	0.3
Clean/dirty	9	1	12	0	0.0
Weak/strong	1	15	8	8	5.6*
Yielding/unyielding	0	19	18	2	28.2*
Disreputable/reputable	7	5	0	17	10.1*
Brave/cowardly	13	4	8	5	0.2
Aggressive/defensive	18	2	2	18	22.5*
Conservative/liberal	12	5	7	11	2.4
Complex/simple	10	5	8	5	0.0
Warm/cold	3	16	15	1	18.1*

*Significant at or beyond the .05 level.
[a]Center scale point not included, so frequencies do not necessarily add to 40.

Table G. High Mach Expects Competitive Other: Disconfirmed
(Solid Line = Second Impression   Dotted Line = Third Impression)

good	bad*
passive	active*
dishonest	honest*
sensitive	insensitive*
light	heavy
generous	selfish*
hostile	peaceful*
competent	incompetent*
soft	hard*
wise	foolish
suspicious	trusting*
constrained	free
awful	nice
open	closed*
masculine	feminine
cooperative	competitive*
fast	slow*
small	large
clean	dirty
weak	strong*
yielding	unyielding*
disreputable	reputable
brave	cowardly
aggressive	defensive*
conservative	liberal
complex	simple*
warm	cold*

*Indicates significant change.

80

Table H. Low Mach Expects Competitive Other: Disconfirmed
(Solid Line = Second Impression   Dotted Line = Third Impression)

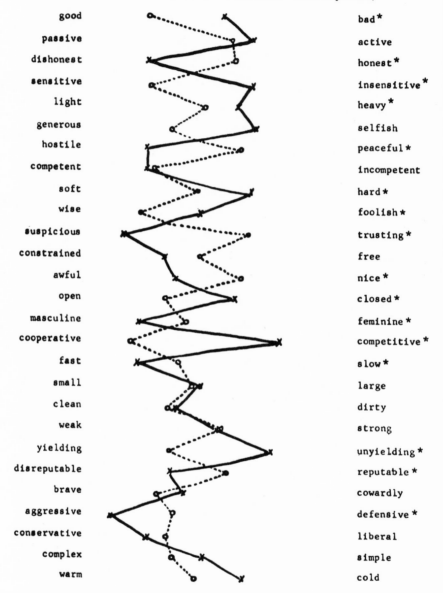

good	bad*
passive	active
dishonest	honest*
sensitive	insensitive*
light	heavy*
generous	selfish
hostile	peaceful*
competent	incompetent
soft	hard*
wise	foolish*
suspicious	trusting*
constrained	free
awful	nice*
open	closed*
masculine	feminine*
cooperative	competitive*
fast	slow*
small	large
clean	dirty
weak	strong
yielding	unyielding*
disreputable	reputable*
brave	cowardly
aggressive	defensive*
conservative	liberal
complex	simple
warm	cold

81

Table I. High Mach Expects Cooperative Other: Disconfirmed
(Solid Line = Second Impression   Dotted Line = Third Impression)

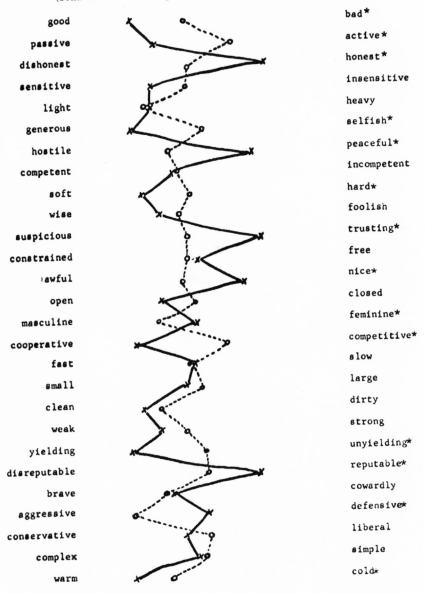

good	bad*
passive	active*
dishonest	honest*
sensitive	insensitive
light	heavy
generous	selfish*
hostile	peaceful*
competent	incompetent
soft	hard*
wise	foolish
suspicious	trusting*
constrained	free
awful	nice*
open	closed
masculine	feminine*
cooperative	competitive*
fast	slow
small	large
clean	dirty
weak	strong
yielding	unyielding*
disreputable	reputable*
brave	cowardly
aggressive	defensive*
conservative	liberal
complex	simple
warm	cold*

82

Table J. Low Mach Expects Coöperative Other: Disconfirmed
(Solid Line = Second Impression   Dotted Line = Third Impression)

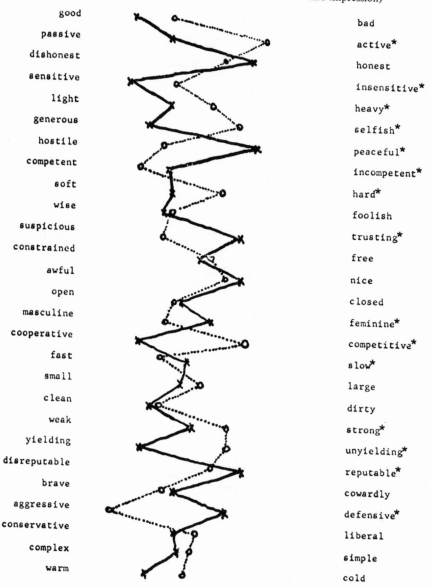

good	bad
passive	active*
dishonest	honest
sensitive	insensitive*
light	heavy*
generous	selfish*
hostile	peaceful*
competent	incompetent*
soft	hard*
wise	foolish
suspicious	trusting*
constrained	free
awful	nice
open	closed
masculine	feminine*
cooperative	competitive*
fast	slow*
small	large
clean	dirty
weak	strong*
yielding	unyielding*
disreputable	reputable*
brave	cowardly
aggressive	defensive*
conservative	liberal
complex	simple
warm	cold

Appendix I

Opinion Inventory (Form XX)

Name_____ Birth Date__/__/__

    Listed below are a number of statements. Each represents a commonly held opinion and there are no right or wrong answers. You will probably disagree with some items and agree with others. We are interested in the extent to which you agree or disagree with such matters of opinion.

    Read each statement carefully. Then indicate the extent to which you agree or disagree by circling one of the numbers in front of each statement. The numbers and their meaning are indicated below:

If you *agree strongly*	circle + 3
If you *agree somewhat*	circle + 2
If you *agree slightly*	circle + 1
If you *disagree slightly*	circle − 1
If you *disagree somewhat*	circle − 2
If you *disagree strongly*	circle − 3

    First impressions are usually best in such matters. Read each statement, decide if you agree or disagree and the strength of your opinion, and then circle the appropriate number in front of the statement. *Give your opinion on every statement.*

    If you find that the numbers to be used in answering do not adequately indicate your own opinion, use the one which is closest to the way you feel.

84

-3 -2 -1 +1 +2 +3   1. Never tell anyone the real reason you did something unless it is useful to do so.

-3 -2 -1 +1 +2 +3   2. The best way to handle people is to tell them what they want to hear.

-3 -2 -1 +1 +2 +3   3. One should take action only when sure it is morally right.

-3 -2 -1 +1 +2 +3   4. Most people are basically good and kind.

-3 -2 -1 +1 +2 +3   5. It is safest to assume that all people have a vicious streak and it will come out when they are given a chance.

-3 -2 -1 +1 +2 +3   6. Honesty is the best policy in all cases.

-3 -2 -1 +1 +2 +3   7. There is no excuse for lying to someone else.

-3 -2 -1 +1 +2 +3   8. Generally speaking, men won't work hard unless they are forced to do so.

-3 -2 -1 +1 +2 +3   9. All in all, it is better to be humble and honest than to be important and dishonest.

-3 -2 -1 +1 +2 +3   10. When you ask someone to do something for you, it is best to give the real reasons for wanting it rather than giving reasons which carry more weight.

-3 -2 -1 +1 +2 +3   11. Most people who get ahead in the world lead clean, moral lives.

-3 -2 -1 +1 +2 +3   12. Anyone who completely trusts anyone else is asking for trouble.

-3 -2 -1 +1 +2 +3   13. The biggest difference between most criminals and other people is that the criminals are stupid enough to get caught.

-3 -2 -1 +1 +2 +3   14. Most men are brave.

-3 -2 -1 +1 +2 +3   15. It is wise to flatter important people.

-3 -2 -1 +1 +2 +3   16. It is possible to be good in all respects.

-3 -2 -1 +1 +2 +3   17. Barnum was wrong when he said that there's a sucker born every minute.

-3 -2 -1 +1 +2 +3   18. It is hard to get ahead without cutting corners here and there.

-3 -2 -1 +1 +2 +3   19. People suffering from incurable diseases should have the choice of being put painlessly to death.

-3 -2 -1 +1 +2 +3   20. Most men forget more easily the death of their own father than the loss of their property.

Appendix II

Mach V Attitude Inventory

You will find 20 groups of statements listed below. Each group is composed of three statements. Each statement refers to a way of thinking about people or things in general. They reflect opinions and not matters of fact — there are no "right" or "wrong" answers and different people have been found to agree with different statements.

Please read each of the three statements in each group. Then decide *first* which of the statements is *most true* or comes the *closest* to describing your own beliefs. Mark a plus (+) in the space before this statement.

Next, decide which of the remaining two statements is *most false* or is the *farthest* from your own beliefs. Place a zero (0) in the space before this statement.

Here is an example:

___ A. It is easy to persuade people but hard to keep them persuaded.

_+_ B. Theories that run counter to common sense are a waste of time.

_0_ C. It is only common sense to go along with what other people are doing and not be too different.

In this case, statement B would be the one you believe in most strongly and A and C would be ones that are not as characteristic of your opinion. Statement C would be the one you believe in least strongly and is least characteristic of your beliefs.

You will find some of the choices easy to make; others will be quite difficult. Do not fail to make a choice no matter how hard it may be. You will mark *two* statements in each group of three — the one that comes the closest to your own beliefs with a + and the one farthest from your beliefs with a 0. The remaining statement should be left unmarked.

86

DO NOT OMIT ANY GROUPS OF STATEMENTS.

Name _____ Birth Date:__/__/__

__A. It takes more imagination to be a successful criminal than a successful business man.
1.__B. The phrase, "the road to hell is paved with good intentions" contains a lot of truth.
__C. Most men forget more easily the death of their father than the loss of their property.

__A. Men are more concerned with the car they drive than with the clothes their wives wear.
2.__B. It is very important that imagination and creativity in children be cultivated.
C. People suffering from incurable diseases should have the choice of being put painlessly to death.

__A. Never tell anyone the real reason you did something unless it is useful to do so.
3.__B. The well-being of the individual is the goal that should be worked for before anything else.
__C. Once a truly intelligent person makes up his mind about the answer to a problem he rarely continues to think about it.

__A. People are getting so lazy and self-indulgent that it is bad for our country.
4.__B. The best way to handle people is to tell them what they want to hear.
C. It would be a good thing if people were kinder to others less fortunate than themselves.

__A. Most people are basically good and kind.
5.__B. The best criterion for a wife or husband is compatibility – other characteristics are nice but not essential.
__C. Only after a man has gotten what he wants from life should he concern himself with the injustices in the world.

__A. Most people who get ahead in the world lead clean, moral lives.
6.__B. Any man worth his salt shouldn't be blamed for putting his career above his family.
__C. People would be better off if they were concerned less with how to do things and more with what to do.

___A. A good teacher is one who points out unanswered questions rather than gives explicit answers.

7.___B. When you ask someone to do something for you, it is best to give the real reasons for wanting it rather than giving reasons which might carry more weight.

___C. A person's job is the best single guide as to the sort of person he is.

___A. The construction of such monumental works as the Egyptian pyramids was worth the enslavement of the workers who built them.

8.___B. Once a way of handling problems has been worked out it is best to stick with it.

___C. One should take action only when sure that it is morally right.

___A. The world would be a much better place to live in if people would let the future take care of itself and concern themselves only with enjoying the present.

9.___B. It is wise to flatter important people.

___C. Once a decision has been made, it is best to keep changing it as new circumstances arise.

___A. It is a good policy to act as if you are doing the things you do because you have no other choice.

10.___B. The biggest difference between most criminals and other people is that criminals are stupid enough to get caught.

___C. Even the most hardened and vicious criminal has a spark of decency somewhere within him.

___A. All in all, it is better to be humble and honest than to be important and dishonest.

11.___B. A man who is able and willing to work hard has a good chance of succeeding in whatever he wants to do.

___C. If a thing does not help us in our daily lives, it isn't very important.

___A. A person shouldn't be punished for breaking a law which he thinks is unreasonable.

12.___B. Too many criminals are not punished for their crime.

___C. There is no excuse for lying to someone else.

___A. Generally speaking, men won't work hard unless they're forced to do so.

13.___B. Every person is entitled to a second chance, even after he commits a serious mistake.

___C. People who can't make up their minds aren't worth bothering about.

___A. A man's first responsibility is to his wife, not his mother.

14.___B. Most men are brave.

___C. It's best to pick friends that are intellectually stimulating rather than ones it is comfortable to be around.

___A. There are very few people in the world worth concerning oneself about.

15.___B. It is hard to get ahead without cutting corners here and there.

___C. A capable person motivated for his own gain is more useful to society than a well-meaning but ineffective one.

___A. It is best to give others the impression that you can change your mind easily.

16.___B. It is a good working policy to keep on good terms with everyone.

___C. Honesty is the best policy in all cases.

___A. It is possible to be good in all respects.

17.___B. To help oneself is good; to help others even better.

___C. War and threats of war are unchangeable facts of human life.

___A. Barnum was probably right when he said that there's at least one sucker born every minute.

18.___B. Life is pretty dull unless one deliberately stirs up some excitement.

___C. Most people would be better off if they controlled their emotions.

___A. Sensitivity to the feelings of others is worth more than poise in social situations.

19.___B. The ideal society is one where everybody knows his place and accepts it.

___C. It is safest to assume that all people have a vicious streak and it will come out when they are given a chance.

___A. People who talk about abstract problems usually don't know what they are talking about.

20.___B. Anyone who completely trusts anyone else is asking for trouble.

___C. It is essential for the functioning of a democracy that everyone vote.

Appendix III

Instructions for Card Sorting

Your task in this phase of the study is to sort the statements contained on the cards in front of you. The procedure is essentially simple, if cumbersome. Look through the 36 cards. You are to sort these statements into a row of 9 categories placing at one end of the row those cards you consider *most characteristic* or *representative* with respect to yourself and at the other end, those cards you believe to be *most uncharacteristic* or *unrepresentative* with respect to yourself.

A convenient method of sorting is first to form three stacks of cards – those items seen as characteristic being placed on one side, those statements seen as uncharacteristic being placed on the other side, and those cards remaining falling in between. No attention need be paid to the number of cards falling into each of these three groupings at this time. When the three piles of cards have been established, they may be further divided, this time into their proper proportions. The number of cards to be placed in each category follows:

Category	No. of Cards	Label of Category
9	2	extremely characteristic or representative
8	3	quite characteristic or representative
7	4	fairly characteristic or representative
6	5	somewhat characteristic or representative
5	8	about equally characteristic & uncharacteristic
4	5	somewhat uncharacteristic or unrepresentative
3	4	fairly uncharacteristic or unrepresentative
2	3	quite uncharacteristic or unrepresentative
1	2	extremely uncharacteristic or unrepresentative

You may feel some resentment at the limitations imposed upon you by the fixed arrangement of statements. However, it is necessary to do this in order to achieve comparable results from one person to another.

Appendix IV

Summary of Product Values

BLACK PRODUCT = 3 cents each.

BLUE PRODUCT = 6 cents each if paired with the other person's blue product. If not paired it is worth 1 cent.

RED PRODUCT = 6 cents each if used to attack other person and if the other person is not fully defended by green products.

GREEN PRODUCT = 6 cents each if, when attacked by the other person, you have more greens than he has reds.

NOTE: An attack is made by transferring an orange marker and saying the word "attack."

An attack uses up the attacker's reds and wipes out the other's greens. But the attacker's greens and the other's reds are left intact.

You may use the remainder of this page for any calculations you might wish to make:

Appendix V

Production Schedule for Stooge:

Round	Black	Blue	Red	Green
1	1	0	0	0
2	1	1	0	0
3	1	1	1	0
4	1	1	1	1
5	1	1	2	1
6	1	1	3	1
7	1	1	3	2
INSPECTION				
8	1	2	3	2
9	1	2	4	2
10	1	2	4	2
11	1	2	0	3
12	1	3	0	3
13	1	3	0	4
14	1	3	0	5
INSPECTION				
15	1	4	0	5
16	2	4	0	5
17	3	4	0	5
18	3	5	0	5
19	3	6	0	5
20	3	6	0	6
21	3	7	0	6
INSPECTION				

Round	Black	Blue	Red	Green
22	3	7	0	7
23	4	7	0	7
24	4	8	0	7
25	4	9	0	7
26	4	9	0	8
27	4	9	0	9
28	4	10	0	9
INSPECTION				
29	4	10	0	10
30	5	10	0	10
31	6	10	0	10
32	6	11	0	10
33	6	12	0	10
34	7	12	0	10
35	7	12	0	11

ATTACK occurs in tenth round

Appendix VI

Scale Values of Q Sort

"Most Characteristic," "Neutral," and "Least Characteristic" descriptions of the High Mach personality based on *California Q Sorts* consensus among four observers. The mean scale value is given at the left of each item. 9.0 = most characteristic; 1.0 = least characteristic.

Scale Value	Descriptions
	"Most Characteristic"
9.0	Is guileful and deceitful, manipulative, opportunistic.
9.0	Characteristically pushes and tries to stretch limits; sees what he can get away with.
9.0	Is power oriented; values power in self and others.
8.75	Is critical, skeptical, not easily impressed.
8.25	Is basically distrustful of people in general; questions their motivations.
	"Neutral"
5.0	Is personally charming.
5.0	Is physically attractive; good-looking.
5.0	Tends to perceive many different contexts in sexual terms; eroticizes situations.
5.0	Is concerned with own body and the adequacy of its physiological functioning.
5.0	Appears to have a high degree of intellectual capacity.
	"Least Characteristic"
1.5	Seeks reassurance from others.
1.5	*Genuinely* submissive; accepts domination comfortably.
1.5	Behaves in a giving way toward others.
1.25	Behaves in a sympathetic or considerate manner.
1.0	Is moralistic.

Appendix VII

Personality Description

Now that you have received information regarding the new person you are to describe this person on the following questionnaire. In completing this questionnaire please make your judgments on the basis of the impression you now have of this new person. You are to rate this person on each of the following scales.

Here is how you are to use these scales:
If you feel that this person is *very closely related* to one end of the scale, you should place your check mark as follows:

fair __X__ : ____ : ____ : ____ : ____ : ____ : ____ unfair

or

fair ____ : ____ : ____ : ____ : ____ : ____ : _X_ unfair

If you feel that this person is *quite closely related* to one or the other end of the scale (but not extremely), you should place your check mark as follows:

strong ____ : _X_ : ____ : ____ : ____ : ____ : ____ weak

or

strong ____ : ____ : ____ : ____ : ____ : _X_ : ____ weak

If the person seems only *slightly related* to one side as opposed to the other side (but is not really neutral), then you should check as follows:

active ____ : ____ : _X_ : ____ : ____ : ____ : ____ passive

or

active ____ : ____ : ____ : ____ : _X_ : ____ : ____ passive

If you consider this person to be neutral on the scale, both sides of the scale *equally associated* with this person, or if the scale is *completely irrelevant*, unrelated to this person, then you should place your check mark in the middle space:

safe ____ : ____ : ____ : _x_ : ____ : ____ : ____ dangerous

Make each item a separate and independent judgment. Work at a fairly high speed through this test. Do not worry or puzzle over individual items. It is your first impressions, the immediate "feelings" about this person, that we want. On the other hand, please do not be careless, because we want your true impressions.

PLACE YOUR CHECK MARKS IN THE MIDDLE OF SPACES AND DO NOT OMIT ANY.

good	:	:	:	:	:	:	bad
passive	:	:	:	:	:	:	active
dishonest	:	:	:	:	:	:	honest
sensitive	:	:	:	:	:	:	insensitive
light	:	:	:	:	:	:	heavy
generous	:	:	:	:	:	:	selfish
hostile	:	:	:	:	:	:	peaceful
competent	:	:	:	:	:	:	incompetent
soft	:	:	:	:	:	:	hard
wise	:	:	:	:	:	:	foolish
suspicious	:	:	:	:	:	:	trusting
constrained	:	:	:	:	:	:	free
awful	:	:	:	:	:	:	nice
open	:	:	:	:	:	:	closed
masculine	:	:	:	:	:	:	feminine
cooperative	:	:	:	:	:	:	competitive
fast	:	:	:	:	:	:	slow
small	:	:	:	:	:	:	large
clean	:	:	:	:	:	:	dirty
weak	:	:	:	:	:	:	strong
yielding	:	:	:	:	:	:	unyielding
disreputable	:	:	:	:	:	:	reputable
brave	:	:	:	:	:	:	cowardly
aggressive	:	:	:	:	:	:	defensive
conservative	:	:	:	:	:	:	liberal
complex	:	:	:	:	:	:	simple
warm	:	:	:	:	:	:	cold

Strategy Description

In the production task which you performed earlier and are about to perform again with a new person, three basic orientations generally guide a person's production. Thus, there are three preferences toward the task that the person you have just described might take. They are:

A) The person could prefer that in the final outcome of the task the sum of his wealth *and* yours is the greatest possible sum of the payoff. A person operating with this orientation would produce blue products most often.

OR

B) The person could prefer that in the final outcome of the task the sum of his wealth is *greater than* yours in terms of the sum of the final payoff. A person operating with this orientation would produce red products and attack most often.

OR

C) The person could prefer that in the final outcome of the task the sum of his wealth is greatest *regardless* of your outcome. Thus, he would be producing as though he were alone. A person operating with this orientation would produce black products most often.

Now, knowing what you do about the new person, estimate what per cent of the time this person will make products with each of the above orientations. Remember that the person may make products under any combination of the above orientations, or the person may simply produce under one of the orientations. Give your first estimate. Do not worry or puzzle over your estimate.

Orientation A____%
Orientation B____%
Orientation C____%

Be sure your estimate(s) = 100%

Appendix IX

Construction of the Mach Scales

A group of 20 items, based on the writings of Machiavelli, has been developed by Christie.[1] The items are designed to measure an orientation toward viewing others impersonally and as objects to be manipulated. For use in Likert format, the keying of the items was counterbalanced so that subjects cannot obtain either high or low scores simply by consistently agreeing, disagreeing, randomly vacillating between extremes, or cautiously avoiding all extremes. Later, a forced choice scale using the same 20 items was developed to control for socially desirable or undesirable responding. Each Mach item is presented as one of triad of items, controlled for social desirability rating, from which subjects must choose one and reject another. In contrast to the fairly obvious intent of the Likert scale, the forced choice scale provides a disguised measure of Machiavellianism. Simultaneous use of both scales, then, should result in more accurate estimates of subjects' Machiavellianism.

The development of the Mach Scales and early studies in which they were used have been summarized by Christie. Split-half and test-retest estimates of the Likert Scale, called Mach IV, have averaged in the .70's; those for Mach V, the forced choice scale, have averaged in the .60's. Empirical results have been consistent with the concept of Machiavellianism, and correlations between Mach Scale scores and behavioral indices support the construct validity of the Scales. (For copies of the Mach scales see Appendices I and II.)

Later studies by Christie (unpublished) have shown that the scale measures of Machiavellianism have behavioral supports; for example, it was found that high "Machs" more readily manipulated other undergraduates than did their counterparts.

---

[1] R. Christie, Impersonal interpersonal orientations and behavior. *Research Proposal.* NSF. 1962.

96

Appendix X

Q Sort Selection

Having selected the disposition of Machiavellianism and having made the decision to try to create a similar impression in the subjects, the selection of statements followed from earlier work on the development of the Mach scales.

In an unpublished report Geis, Christie, and Nelson[1] and another assistant independently completed Block's[2] California Q Sort to describe the "typical high scorer." The second author sorted the 100 statements primarily on the basis of theory and secondarily from findings of previous studies; the experimenter primarily on the basis of observations in the pilot study and secondarily from knowledge of theory and previous results. The two observers almost exclusively sorted on the basis of expectations and results specific to the situation used. The six intercorrelations ranged from .53 to .78, with a median of .62. Most of the major discrepancies reflected different levels of interpretation by the different sorters. Some of the items could legitimately be classified toward one end of the scale to describe the high Mach as he appears to others.

Appendix VI lists the five "most characteristic" descriptions (items with mean scale values above 8.0); five "neutral" characteristics (those on which there was complete consensus among raters in assigning them to the neutral category); and five "least characteristic" descriptions (items with mean scale values below 2.0). These consensual descriptions again reflect the cold, amoral, and detached personal responsiveness of the High Mach, and his covertly aggressive willingness and ability to manipulate others.

In addition to these statements, thirty others were selected from the California Q sort. In a pilot study the forty-five statements were divided into three sets of 15 each. The first set of fifteen which contained the five high Mach

---

[1] L. Geis, R. Christie, and C. Nelson, *On Machiavellianism*. (Mimeo), 1964. Dept. Soc. Psychol., Columbia University.

[2] J. Block, *The Q-Sort method in personality assessment and psychiatric research.* Springfield, Illinois: Charles C. Thomas, 1961.

statements from Appendix VI was designated as being characteristic of a hypothetical individual. Similarly the five neutral statements were embedded in a set of fifteen designated neutral statements and the five uncharacteristic were embedded in a set of fifteen statements. The entire forty-five statements were placed on a sheet of paper which purported to be the way an individual had assigned the statements to himself. Two such sheets were constructed, one of which reversed the fifteen statements designated characteristic with the fifteen uncharacteristic. These sheets were administered to a small group of people who described the hypothetical person on a semantic differential format. The two sheets elicited different profiles. Next, the entire forty-five statements were used in a pilot experiment and then reduced through an item analysis to thirty statements. Finally, six statements were added as fillers with the intention of selecting statements which would be unrelated to Machiavellianism and interpersonal bargaining. For instance, statements such as, "I enjoy photography," and "I find it pleasurable to listen to piano music," were selected. The list of thirty-six items is contained in Table 3.

Appendix XI

Experimenter Expectancy Effects: A Case Study

This study is concerned with the possibility of expectancy effects within the Lake experiment. The paradigm for such studies usually calls for two or more groups of Es, each of which has been led to expect a different set of results. Here we shall use one E under two different conditions. In one condition the E knows the S's Mach score (early Ss) and in the second condition he does not have this piece of information (late Ss).

If expectancy effects are operating in this experiment then the behavior of those Ss whose Mach scores were known to the E at the time of the experiment should conform to the predicted behavior significantly more often than the behavior of those Ss whose Mach scores were not known to the E at that time. If expectancy effects are not operating then there should not be a significant difference between the behavior of the two groups.

To test the hypothesis about expectancy effects, the behavior of Ss during the first seven rounds of the second game will be analyzed. At this time there has been sufficient opportunity for the Ss to learn the game, to have certain types of behavior reinforced (if this is to happen at all), and to act in light of the impression which was created for the second game before this impression is either confirmed or disconfirmed (which happens after the seventh round).

The two conditions in which the E's predictions are most clear, and therefore most likely to be vulnerable to expectancy effects, are the high Machs in the competitive-expectation condition and the low Machs in the cooperative-expectation condition. We will therefore examine these two conditions.

It is expected that high Machs would behave aggressively, producing more red products and/or attacking often when in the competitive condition. It is further expected that Lake would try to influence those high Machs he had identified to produce more reds and/or attack more often than those high Machs he did not know about — if expectancy effects are operating. The mean number of reds produced by the high Machs who were not identified was 1.27; the mean number of reds produced by the high Machs who were identified to the E was

1.70. The difference between the means yielded a t-score of +.0052. The critical value was 2.093. Clearly, the difference between the means is not significant and we cannot reject the null hypothesis that $\bar{x}_1 = \bar{x}_2$.

In the cooperative situation Lake expects the low Machs to play cooperatively. Therefore, if expectancy effects are operating here we would expect the low Machs Lake had identified to produce significantly more "blues" (the cooperative product) than the low Machs he had not identified. The mean number of blue products produced by those low Machs run without knowledge of the Mach scores was 3.09; the mean number of blues produced by those run with this knowledge was 1.57. The t-score was 0.5371. The critical value for this test was 2.120. Again we cannot reject the null hypothesis.

Thus we may conclude that expectancy effects are not operating in this experiment.

Although it has been shown that experimenter expectancy effects are not operating in this experiment, it may be fruitful to examine the possible sources of such bias and the stops which can be taken to guard against them. It was found that restriction of visual cues accounted for eighty percent of the variance of bias magnitude in one experiment. Lake has very little contact of this nature with his subjects; directions are given over the public address system from a prerecorded tape while Lake observes his subject through one-way glass. His few contacts with the subjects are brief and business-like, e.g. E walks into room and picks up the completed Mach sheets and leaves. Another possible source of bias is giving subjects instructions which differ in tone and/or emphasis. This has been avoided by use of the tape recorder to insure that all Ss receive precisely the same set of directions. There are two other possible sources of bias: answering S's questions and giving feedback on the S's production after each seven rounds.

In observing Lake during the experiment I found that he gave the feedback in the same manner each time, with all subjects. He told each subject in a flat unemotional tone, how many of each type product he had made and how many of each type product his "opponent" had made. The order S_1 or S_2 was always the same and arranged in advance.

In answering his subjects' questions Lake usually paraphrased the directions which had been given on the tape. It is felt that these answers were always straightforward and not intended to bias the subjects.

Thus it would appear that Lake took steps, consciously, to avoid a situation in which expectancy effects would be possible and that he did not change his behavior, either consciously or unconsciously, so as to influence his subjects' behavior in the direction which would support his hypothesis.

Ella Lasky

Scale Values Indicating Relevance of each Statement as Determined by Ten Independent Judges

18 Least Relevant			*18 Most Relevant*		
Statement Number	Scale Value	Number Choosing	Statement Number	Scale Value	Number Choosing
1	5.0	(2)	3	5.7	(4)
2	0.0	(0)	5	7.5	(7)
4	0.0	(0)	9	5.7	(7)
6	5.1	(2)	10	6.8	(7)
7	0.0	(0)	11	6.4	(7)
8	5.0	(1)	12	6.5	(7)
14	5.5	(4)	13	8.2	(7)
16	0.0	(0)	15	6.9	(7)
17	5.0	(2)	19	7.9	(7)
18	5.0	(1)	20	5.0	(5)
21	0.0	(0)	23	7.1	(7)
22	0.0	(0)	25	6.7	(4)
24	0.0	(0)	28	5.5	(6)
26	0.0	(0)	29	6.5	(6)
27	0.0	(0)	30	6.2	(7)
32	0.0	(0)	31	8.0	(7)
33	0.0	(0)	35	6.8	(5)
34	5.0	(2)	36	5.8	(7)

Appendix XIII

Subject Sources

Source	Age Range	Number
Vocational High School	17–30	5
Undergraduates		
Columbia	17–19	7
Hunter	17–21	6
Graduates		
B. A. Complete	18–33	30
M. A. Complete	28–44	12
Actors Equity	20–59	20
TOTAL		80